Torsten Olaf Enge · Carl Friedrich Schröer

Garden Architecture in Europe

1450–1800

From the villa garden of the Italian Renaissance

to the English landscape garden

Photographs by
Martin Claßen · Hans Wiesenhofer

Benedikt Taschen

ILLUSTRATION FRONT COVER:
Stowe, Buckinghamshire, England
View from the Greek temple over the Greek valley

ILLUSTRATION BACK COVER:
Villa d'Este, Tivoli, Italy
Dragon or Wheel of Fire Fountain

ILLUSTRATION PAGE 1:
Schwetzingen, Germany
Pan sculpture

ILLUSTRATION PAGES 6/7:
Sanspareil, Bayreuth, Germany
Ruin and grotto theatre in the park

© 1992 Benedikt Taschen Verlag GmbH,
Hohenzollernring 53, D-5000 Köln 1
Editor and production: Rolf Taschen, Uta Klotz, Cologne
English translation: Ailsa Mattaj
Printed in Germany
ISBN 3-8228-0540-8
GB

Contents

Gardens – Models of a better world

by Carl Friedrich Schröer

Paradise and Utopia

In the beginning was paradise. The age-old myth of the Garden of Eden reflects a fundamental human longing. In paradise, the first humans lived in perfect peace. They knew neither illness nor death, neither drudgery nor poverty; they were free from sexual repression and oppressive rule. The story of paradise told in the Book of Genesis (Genesis = origin) symbolizes mankind's dream of life in mythical accord with nature. From time immemorial, the setting for this natural, harmonious way of life has been the garden.

This ancient dream was soon given both a shape and a name: *"pairi-dae 'za"*. This Old Persian word simply meant "walled", and thus says nothing about what lay in the separate, protected space within. The word "paradise" which our own language has inherited from the Old Persian may be translated as "pleasure garden" or "garden of delight". The image of the walled garden has thus always been the setting for man's longed-for victory over human frailty and imperfection. From this comes the idea of the garden as an Utopian ideal which takes a long-past stage of human development as the model for a better, happier future.

The biblical story of paradise symbolically describes an original and thus completely natural way of life which is supposed to have been open to mankind in the beginning, or at least before history began, and which promises – at the end of time – the restoration of a kingdom of perfect harmony. This ancient Judaeo-Christian model of a better world (which has its parallels in many other cultures) takes a "natural" but lost epoch as the basis upon which to structure, as a beautiful counterpart, a hopeful future – a model for that promised age of all-embracing bliss to be regained at the end of history.

Whether the Garden of Eden ever really existed, what it looked like and where it was located are irrelevant factors in its history. The Garden of Eden has been an inexhaustible model, prototype and distant goal for the planners of large gardens throughout the centuries precisely because it exists only as a literary myth. It is mankind's oldest dream – of life in paradise, of freedom from care, of good health and perpetual happiness – that influences garden architects rather than the sparse descriptions of historical gardens in ancient Persia, Mesopotamia or Anatolia.

The garden has always meant structured yearning, a sentimental return to a golden age and at the same time a step towards Utopia. It represents an attempt to recover a lost paradise on earth and to anticipate the promised kingdom of heaven. The path to this goal is one of reconciliation with nature. This reconciliation can only be successful within the sphere of art. Only within the order of this autonomous sphere can nature once more become beautiful. Here it is neither uneven and stony like farmland, nor rough and dangerous like a wilderness. Gardens unite artificial and natural beauty, embracing all the natural elements – water, light, air,

Chivalrous scene in a garden

Sculpture in the
Klessheim palace gardens, Austria

9

growth – and making them elements of art. Every effort devoted to garden design becomes a mirror of the longing for happiness in harmony with nature. More important than its usefulness as a source of protection, food, medicines and reserve supplies is the garden's ability to provide moments of pleasurable leisure. The dusty earth of everyday life, the thorns and thistles of the workaday world are excluded from the garden of delights. In a garden, the mythical Utopia of peaceful, beautiful nature almost becomes reality. Garden design, like poetry, literature and painting, has always preferred to use distant models which elude critical examination and thus incur no risk of disappointment. The models were always unknown islands of desire, distant not only in space but also in time. Unencumbered by concrete, historical limitations, the imagination could develop beyond the crippling confines of reality. Art and myth have created many such paradises: Elysium, Hesperides, Arcadia, and above all islands: Atlantis, the Isle of the Blessed, Ithaca, Orplid, Avalon, Cythera, Sicily, Capri, Mauritius and Tahiti, the subtropical jungle and the land of milk and honey. Even America, the Swiss Alps and finally the cosmos have been transformed into faraway, Utopian landscapes. Above all, these paradises are artificial, from the earliest myths through to futuristic science fiction – extrapolations, dreams and fantasy rather than concrete places to be found on a map. But no dream world, no island – no matter how fantastic – can exist without reference to reality. Utopia, the nowhereland, has thus always been the goal of human longing unfulfilled in reality. Gardens likewise are a product of the yearning which grows from the humiliations and dashed hopes of daily life, and are thus the reflection and counter-image of a more beautiful world. Designed to bridge borders, gardens shed light on the historical reality of their creation and creators. Like all Utopias, they criticize a concrete political situation, social relationships, constraints and shortcomings.

The dream of paradise encompasses both intimacy and Utopia: daydream, the escape into the idyllic, a low value placed on reality, and at the same time a new departure, a will for change and a desire for freedom. Strength grows out of the beautiful dream, fantasy becomes power, and human freedom triumphs precisely where it must bow to necessity. If we examine Utopias throughout the ages, the optimistic and the pessimistic, those set in a bygone golden era and those set in the far future, we can also identify the powerful thrust towards political change and revolution, the points in the course of history where desires sought to become reality.

Arcadia – the secularized paradise

Arcadia is the other, no less influential point of reference in garden history, a sort of secularized paradise. Adam and Eve do not discover sin in Arcadia; instead, shepherds play the pipes of Pan. God the Father does not watch over the actions of his creatures in Arcadia; rather, a god with goat's legs by the name of Pan is up to his mischief, scaring the shepherds dozing in the midday sun or pursuing timid nymphs. Whereas the Bible story of Paradise represents a positive vision which seeks to defeat heathen polytheism, Arcadia became, during the Renaissance, a Utopian equivalent which eulogized an existence that was pre-Christian and close to nature.

Arcadia became the dream country of modern history, consciously looking back to the ancient world in order to devise a brighter future.

Here, too, is a longing for mystical reunion with nature, this time in a classical shape. The peaceful, hilly countryside of Arcadia was – it was thought – scattered with buildings, grotoes, ruins and temples in the antique style. Since the Renaissance, Pan's kingdom, ennobled by classical literature, has served as a model for a natural and yet delightful other world, an idyllic projection in contrast to concrete reality.

Unlike the Garden of Eden, Arcadia can actually be found on the map: a steep, inhospitable chain of hills on the Peloponnese. Is this bleak hill country really supposed to be the Arcadia where shepherds write poetry, the land of love and desire? It has little more in common with the fictitious Arcadia than its name. But it became an ideal destination nevertheless, thanks to its position; it was located sufficiently far from home to represent the dream land which – in view of the poor urban conditions – was so necessary.

The Roman poet Virgil (70–19 B. C.) set his *Eclogues* in a mythical age – the ancient gods of the Greeks appear alongside valiant shepherds – and gave his stories a pastoral setting. The myth of virtuous country life, continually resisting the decadence of the metropolis, began with his Arcadia. But country life, too, is eased and made more pleasant by civilized behaviour and good taste. "In Virgil's Arcadia the shepherds are filled with emotional sensibilities neither all too rustic nor yet too urbanely sophisticated. In the pastoral idyll of Arcadia the calm of the evening is more apparent than daily labour, the cool shade prevails over more rigorous weather, the soft spot by the stream is more eloquent than rugged moun-

Fontana dell'Isolotto in the *Boboli gardens*, Florence, Italy

The Boboli gardens, which lie behind the Palazzo Pitti, are the most famous of the Medici gardens. Among their showpieces is the Isolotto, created by Alfonso Parigi in 1618: an oval pool in the middle of which is set an artificial island with Giovanni da Bologna's ocean fountain.

11

tains. The shepherds spend more time singing and playing the flute than working in the dairy," writes Bruno Snell, describing the merry life of a shepherd, not without irony. "No one makes calculations in Arcadia, in fact in Arcadia no one thinks in any kind of clear and precise way. Everything exists in a shimmer of emotion. The emotion, however, is not wild and passionate; love in particular is mere sentimental yearning."

Arcadia is the land where everyday life is golden; this everyday life is completely artificial. Everything that happens is significant, exalted and essentially the exact opposite of mundane everyday life. A deep chasm separates the artificial world of Arcadia from normal, everyday life. For Arcadia is above all an aesthetic fiction and a Utopian vision of happiness.

The Renaissance revived the theme of Arcadia in a nostalgic mourning for things past. Thus Pan is dead, as in Jacopo Sannazaro's pastoral novel *Arcadia* (1480) and Torquato Tasso's pastoral play *Aminta* (1573), in which melancholic shepherds once more lament a lost Golden Age, an age that was above all a time of free love. For centuries, writers such as Pietro Bembo, Jorge de Montemayor, Miguel de Cervantes and Honoré d'Urfé, and above all painters and etchers from Giorgione to Titian, from Dosso Dossi to Niccolò dell'Abbate, from Annibale Carracci to Nicolas Poussin and Claude Lorrain, from Jean Antoine Watteau and Jean Honoré Fragonard to Hubert Robert competed in their efforts to evoke antiquity as an Arcadian country of shepherds. "Pastoral" became an established genre. Pastoral plays and fashions spread from Italy throughout Europe and every educated person soon felt as at home in the hilly Arcadian landscape, in the world of Galatea and in the realms of Helicon as in the kingdom of classical mythology. And the Arcadian ideal of an ancient, pastoral world was, of course, taken up and promoted at royal courts with aristocratic extravagance.

Contemporary life was transfigured into artistic Utopia: enthusiasm for art left reality behind, and the entire court of the Medici in Florence was transformed into a work of art set in an ideal classical landscape. Three hundred years later, Frederick the Great, an enlightened ruler, transformed sandy moraine in Brandenburg into an "Arcadia in the Brandenburg Marches", and even British constitutional monarchs saw their state as a work of art as late as the 19th century. But the stage was always Arcadia: intimate conviviality in a rural setting as a contrast to the corrupt life at court.

No wonder garden design flourished in such times. It was so very tempting to make the world of Arcadia once more real, to eliminate the fine distinction between illusion and reality, to recreate the scenery of Virgil and Sannazaro and to make striking copies of the pictorial world of Poussin and Lorrain. No wonder garden design became statecraft and sought both to encompass and surpass all other arts.

Arcadia is one of the most influential ideals in modern history. An unattainably distant landscape has been used over the centuries as an allegory of mankind's yearning for a better world, for a life in harmony with the self, with nature and with God. Arcadia is a secularized paradise which represents – in a similar fashion to the Garden of Eden – an idyllic *locus amoenus*, in which a timeless existence of peace, leisure and love is possible, free from the demands of everyday life. There remains one vital difference: Arcadia is not a divine creation with claims to absoluteness. Arcadia is an artistic product; an intermediate realm which lies somewhere between paradise and reality and which contains aspects of both. This causes both the charm and the pain of Arcadian existence. Arcadia is created by mankind as an artistic configuration; it is even possible to live there contendedly for quite some time. And yet pastoral bliss is constantly under threat: pain, suffering and death have penetrated even Arcadia. But not really. Everything remains at the level of feelings and sentiment. Even love is experienced not sensuously but rather longingly. The desire for love, rather than its fulfilment, is the true Arcadian sentiment.

The idealization of the pastoral can already be seen in the bucolic poetry of antiquity. Even in those days the shepherd was an archetype, his way

Garden on the Isola Bella
Lago Maggiore, Italy

of life symbolizing man's closeness to nature. Such a natural, roving existence was intended to recall the former Golden Age. Arcadia was invented by the Roman poet Virgil. But it was only later, during the Renaissance, that bucolic poetry acquired Utopian potential. The land of pastoral musicians was reborn in Sannazaro's *Arcadia* and once again the country of birth was Italy. This key work in European bucolic poetry provides not merely a refuge, an excape from hateful reality; its pastoral symbolism also cloaks Utopian alternative. It is less a paradise for eroto-maniacs than a processing of contemporary history, coupled with the urgent invitation to enter directly the promised alternative world of Arcadia. Like Utopia, the pastoral novel is an invention of the early modern age. Both borrow from predecessors from the age of antiquity, both revive ancient forms as a means of self-legitimation. Sannazaro drew upon Virgil's fictitious pastoral world. He thus set the direction of this literary genre: *Arcadia all'antica*. The shepherds appear in antique clothing, bear Greek or Latin names, while the landscape is decorated with classical architecture and ruins.

From the Renaissance up until the 19th century, Arcadia maintained its position within the history of art. From its origins in poetry and landscape painting it went on to become a leitmotif of modern garden design.

Hypnerotomachia Poliphili

One other novel from this period is worthy of attention: *Hypneroto-machia Poliphili* ("The Strife of Love in a Dream") by Francesco Colonna, which was first published in Venice in 1499. This work is of major significance for the history of ideas in garden design. It contains the fundamental ideas underlying the Renaissance garden in all their purity: a microcosmic gathering together of the whole of nature under the rule of mankind. Hierarchical gradation, strict axiality and geometric order anticipate modern plans of the Ideal City. The book takes the form of a romance and is modelled on predecessors such as Guillaume de Lorris' *Roman de la Rose*, Dante's *Divine Comedy*, and Boccaccio's *Decameron*. Poliphilo (= Polia's lover) describes to his beloved a dream which leads him, in five stages, to union with her. Only in the final stage of the dream do both lovers manage to reach Cythera, Aphrodite's island. Cupid himself rows the couple over the waves in his boat. Once they have arrived on the island they drive in a triumphal chariot to the goddess's shrine, which stands at the very centre of the island of love. Cythera is depicted as an artistically designed garden. The union of the lovers finally takes place in an amphitheatre in the middle of the island: Poliphilo tears a curtain, hymen, which screens the fountain in which Aphrodite bathes.

Colonna equates the desired woman, Polia, with antiquity. It is she who leads Poliphilo on the long route to antiquity. The romance becomes a declaration of love for a former age. The author's main purpose is to offer an impressive picture of the culture, architecture, applied art and fashions of classical antiquity. But Colonna does not restrict himself to sober descriptions of classical antecedents; rather, he seeks to outdo them through the power of his imagination. Thus he invents, for example, a fantasy garden made of glass, one of silk and a third of precious stones.

A stage for the mythology of nature

In the complete design of the gardens of the Renaissance, and even more so in those of Mannerism and the Baroque, iconographical pro-grammes were developed which frequently combined an Arcadian ideal with a stage setting for the mythology of nature. The figures which appear in the gardens, decorating fountains and grottoes or standing in independent groups, are borrowed from ancient tradition, above all from Ovid's *Meta-morphoses*, Virgil's *Eclogues* and – following his rediscovery at the beginning of the 15th century – Lucretius' philosophical work *De rerum natura*.

Ancient mythology regained major significance during the Renaissance; both the figures of the Olympian gods and the grotesque half-castes – demonic crossbreeds of animals, men and gods – personified and preserved the lost wisdom of a classical mysticism and philosophy of nature which it was hoped could be regained. It was believed that the secret, lost knowledge of the ancients was hidden in myth. Mythical figures represented the functioning of the free powers of nature, which it was sought to influence via magic rituals and mystical sculptures. The actual physical location of the figures in a garden was also believed to be of decisive

Garden of the *Villa Lante*, Bagnaia, Italy
Water cascade pouring down a stepped channel into a semicircular pool

Garden of the *Villa Lante*, Bagnaia, Italy

The garden of the Villa Lante is one of the best-preserved Renaissance gardens in Italy. The central axis, bordered at the end of the ornamental garden by two small villas – a peculiarity of this particular garden – connects three areas of approximately equal size.

significance for their energic effectiveness. The central figure in the mythology of nature is Pan, the Greek deity who presides over Arcadia's shepherds and flocks. In ancient Rome he was already fully associated with fauns and satyrs. He is an ever-lascivious hybrid with goat's legs, horns and ears, who usually dwells in a grotto (one reason for the countless grottoes in all the gardens). The complexity of his many roles is astonishing. Pan (Greek for "all") is the personification of the universe, and often seen as a general symbol of nature itself. The god of the shepherds was often to be found in the company of Dionysos (Bacchus), or pursuing nymphs. He invented the shepherd's pipe and knew nature's secrets. As early as the 15th century, Pan had come to symbolize driving natural sexuality and the free, self-sufficient course of nature.

Boccaccio (1313–1375), whose *De Genealogia Deorum Gentilium* remained a standard work up until the 17th century, identified Pan more precisely with *natura naturata*, a lower form of nature which, once created, reproduces itself unaided.

Proportion and beauty

The thirst for a (secret) ancient understanding of nature, and the yearning for the pastoral delights of Arcadia, led during the Renaissance to an enthusiasm for satyrs. Satyrs and nymphs are first and foremost inhabitants of Arcadia – that mythical region which echoes the Golden Age, that paradisaical state of harmony when the gods mixed freely with mortals. The culture of the Renaissance aimed for harmony of form. The philosophical, mathematical and artistic tendencies of the age are contained within the concept of proportion. The new art form, that of garden design, was singularly capable of integrating and exemplifying these different trends. The architectural garden, evidence of a "rational", measurable art, was a guarantee of beauty. All the elements in the architectural garden were subject to a geometrical order in accordance with the accepted laws of proportion.

Beauty is based above all on correspondance with a nature, which was seen as nothing less than absolute, God-given harmony. Indeed, beauty, the "radiance of God's countenance", is equated with love. Thus are revealed the true poles of the axis around which revolve the teachings of Marsilio Ficino (1433–99). The cult of Pan and Venus in the gardens of the Renaissance derives from two sources: the myth of Arcadia and Platonic teachings on Eros. To Plato, Eros was a "demonic" creature, combining the godlike and the human, the world of the intellect and the world of the senses. Eros' conflicting natures forms the motive moment in the Platonic cosmos. In the Neoplatonism of the Florentine Academy love functions in two directions: it is both the compulsive desire of the higher for the lower, of the spiritual for the sensual, and the yearning of the lower for the higher. "It is characteristic of all divine spirits," writes Ficino, "that while they behold the superior, they never cease to look down to that which is inferior and to look after it. This is also a characteristic of our soul, which takes on the care and nurture not just of its own body but of the bodies of all earthly things and of the earth itself." Care and nurture are thus crucial factors. While beauty derives from the material world, it must be shaped by man's free creativity. Nature becomes the medium. Only the artist can reveal the beauty inherent in nature: hence the conclusion that, without the artist, nature is both unattractive and useless – and thus loses its most advantageous characteristics. From this perspective, the art of garden design is the highest expression of nature. In other words: nature only attains ultimate perfection through the caring and nurturing hand of the artist. There is thus no conflict between trimmed hedges, pruned trees or geometrical parterres and nature. The one is simply the raw material which has to be modelled (it would later be called "improved") into beauty. No wonder such a philosophy proved a sweeping success. Particularly, of course, among artists, who now had a decisive role to play in the transformation of nature into art. It was likewise no wonder that artists turned increasingly to garden design, since they could here prove so convincingly to any onlooker how it was possible – in a few "creative" steps – to transform a piece of fallow land into a verdant work of art.

Ficino's elder contemporary, Leon Baptista Alberti, confirms this relationship between art and nature: "The idea of beauty," he states in his major work, *On Architecture* (c. 1452), "arises not so much from the body in which it is found, or from any one of the parts of that body, but much more from itself and from nature, so that its true location is in the mind and in the reason."

According to Alberti, architecture, and in consequence garden architecture, had a particular task to fulfil. It was to imitate the idea of nature

FOLLOWING DOUBLE PAGE:
Garden of the *Villa Lante*, Bagnaia, Italy
Fountain with figures of river gods

17

Garden of the *Villa il Bosco di Fonte Lucente*
Fiesole, Italy

as a whole (and not merely one of its parts). The plan of a park or garden was to be drawn up according to those "natural proportions" by which all of nature's creations are formed. Thus beauty came to be understood as a universal law, governing both nature and the creative artist. The architect, in making his plans, could not employ purely arbitrary proportions, but only those which enabled nature to reach its aesthetic objective. (Thus contemporary opinion saw an unsuccessful building as one in which the laws of natural proportion had not been incorporated.) Natural order (already described by Pythagoras in ancient times), which could be recognized in the harmonies of music, appeared analogously in the proportional designs of Renaissance architecture. Natural order represents universal order and thus natural beauty. When we speak today of an "architectural garden", we mean a garden laid out in perspective, following the laws of proportion or geometry and thus providing a picture of nature as a whole which seeks less to reproduce the "material substance" of nature – leaves, the scent of flowers or the twittering of birds – than to recreate its proportional order. The architectural garden attempts to convey an insight into the internal construction of its beauty.

Ficino's Garden of Intellectuals

"Our age is a golden era which has revived from virtual extinction the liberal arts, grammar, poetry, rhetoric, painting, architecture, sculpture,

Garden of the *Villa il Bosco di Fonte Lucente*
Fiesole, Italy

music and singing to the Orphean lyre. And all this was achieved in Florence". Marsilio Ficino, thus praising his native city in a letter written in 1492 to the Flemish humanist Paul von Middelburg, was merely expressing the general mood of the times. This optimistic conviction of standing on the verge of a better future was the remarkable characteristic of a century which had just overcome the "dark and dreadful times" of the Middle Ages.

The energetic, driving mood of the Renaissance has to be viewed against a backdrop of the disintegration of the mediaeval world order: the decline of those universal forces of order, empire and papacy, the disruption of scholastic education, doubt about the indivisibility of knowledge and belief and the shattering of social and economic structures. The four Riders of the Apocalypse – war, famine, death and plague – had galloped through Europe. The plague alone had left 30 million dead.

In this attempt to recreate the pre-mediaeval – antique – world, both a recollection of the past and the design of an ideal future, lies the Janus-faced nature of the period which we today call the Renaissance. This same period was itself celebrated as the rebirth of the Golden Age, and – for us perhaps surprisingly – the arts were viewed as the pioneering forces behind the general upward turn. The arts were thus allocated an incomparably more important role than in antiquity.

Despite the hardship of their times, the humanists of the 14th century had already placed an astonishing amount of trust in human capabilities:

mankind – if he will only follow ancient examples – is capable of mastering nature. This was an expression of belief in a system of rational thought and of a rational ordering of political and social relationship, a belief in the progress which was to become the propelling force of the modern age.

The increasing interest of the educated Florentine public in Greek philosophy, given impetus by a series of lectures by Byzantine scholars on Platonic ideas, led to the formation of a circle which met regularly in Ficino's Accademia. Ficino later reported that Cosimo de Medici (Cosimo

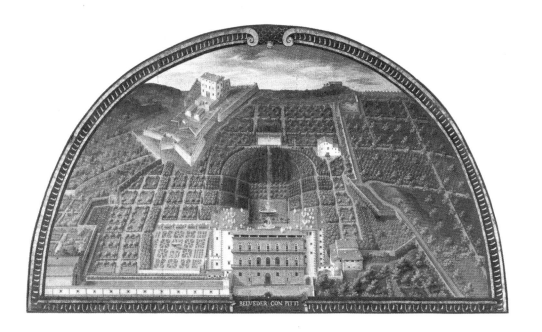

The Boboli gardens with the Palazzo Pitti in Florence
Painting by Giusto Utens, 1599

the Elder), banker, statesman and patron of the arts, had been so impressed by the lectures of the invited scholars that he spontaneously decided to found an academy along antique, Platonic lines. Cosimo made it possible for the youthful Ficino to translate Plato's forgotten works from Greek into Latin and in 1462 made him a present of his country house, the Villa Careggi, which stood on a hillside near Florence.

There the great Greek philosopher was emulated with faithful enthusiasm. It was soon insufficient merely to interpret Plato's writings; his entire life was taken as an example to be copied. Plato, who liked to teach his pupils in his extensive garden, came to be a comprehensive role model for Ficino and his Academy. Thus the garden was seen as a natural part of the Academy and one which came to be regarded as the most noble expression of a humanistic education and a cosmopolitan mind. The link between garden design and a group of scholars was of decisive importance for the design and development of the garden in the modern age. Wherever – in conscious or unconscious imitation of the Florentine humanists – an artistic court, an enlightened princely household or a circle of citizen scholars where to be found, garden design was never far away.

Ficino hoped to do for philosophy what his contemporaries believed Giotto had already succeeded in doing for painting and Dante for poetry. And in fact Platonism became the dominant *Weltanschauung* of the Renaissance: a philosophical Renaissance. Ficino's Neoplatonism became the leading mode of thought, a "Great Power in European culture" (Panofsky). Ficino's Platonism strives to combine the systems of Christian theology and of philosophy. As expressed in the title of his major work, *Theologica Platonica*, he seeks to reconcile scholasticism with Platonism.

The Florentine Academy in Careggi was more than just a group of esoteric scholars. From the very beginning it was a community of friends in the spirit of Plato, a teaching and living community. The rebirth of antiquity was understood principally as a revival of ancient customs and manners. The high points of life at the Academy were the "feast", scholarly banquets whose guests included both the members of the Academy and learned men from various professions. A Platonic "Symposium" was held in Careggi every 7 November, the alleged date of Plato's birth and death, culminating in a celebratory recreation of Platonic tradition – a mixture of banquet and festival. Ficino himself described such a banquet thus: "After the meal, Bernardo Nuzzi seized that book by Plato which has the title *Symposium* or *On love* and recited all the speeches which had been made at the original banquet. After he had finished, he requested that each of his dinner companions should interpret one of the speeches. And everyone agreed."

But Ficino was not content to stop at imitation. Unlike Plato's academy in Athens, his own Florentine successor was to become a universal seat of learning. Its educational programme was directed at all people, regardless of age, profession or background.

With the Accademia Platonica, a programme was formulated which significantly influenced the development of garden design in modern times. In the course of time artistic gardens everywhere were created with an astonishing devotion to the spirit of Humanism and Neoplatonic philosophy. Since the Renaissance, gardens have been more closely associated with knowledge and education than with a purely sensory enjoyment of nature. There is no fundamental reason for this: since the Renaissance, gardens have been viewed as works of art and not merely as enclosed, walled pieces of land to be used by their owners for keeping animals or growing vegetables. With the Renaissance, garden design – like other art forms – was freed from the yoke of utility.

The Medici Villas after Utens

The development of the Tuscan villa garden since the middle of the 15th century can be seen in a unique series of paintings: Giusto Utens, a painter of Flemish extraction, was commissioned by the Grand Duke Ferdinando I de Medici to document all the villas belonging to the House of Medici.

The pictures were painted for the banqueting hall of the Villa La Ferdinanda, built by Buontalenti. They were set into the bays of the hall vaulting hence their lunette form. Today the fourteen paintings hang in the Museo Storico Topografico in Florence (Villa dell'Oriuolo 4).

The fourteen villas with their parks, painted by Utens around 1598 from a bird's eye perspective, give an impressive and informative overview which ranges from the country house of Caffaggiolo, ancestral seat of the Medici since the 14th century, to the Villa Pratolino, a huge complex with pleasure garden which Buontalenti started building in 1570.

While these villa estates belong to the Renaissance period, they display few distinctive garden forms. Neighbouring farm buildings, stables, orchards and olive groves, fields and meadows point to the productive side of the villa. The mainly flat, occasionally slightly hilly ground appears sectionalized into plots. The rectangular plots are planted with fruit trees, in whose shadows flowers, herbs and vegetables doubtless grew. Architecture remained in the background in these gardens. Only close to the house, for instance in the walled *giardino segreto* (secret garden), does the decorative gain a certain significance.

The evolution of the garden from the villa

Garden design derived from the city. And yet its setting remains the countryside. In the city one dreams the "dream of the countryside" – as a happy future and pleasant counterpoint to city life in the palace, town hall, church and commerce. In summer, one leaves the city in order to realize this dream in the "open countryside". Man has dreamed of the country for as long as cities have existed; this dream has been a constant component of the cultural history of the western world since classical antiquity.

This dream was given its first and most lasting shape in Italy: in the villa. Modelled on the *villa rustica* of antiquity, the villa developed during the 14th and 15th centuries from an enclosed, castle-like dwelling into the typical Renaissance villa, whose ideal and composition were to influence garden design until well into the 18th century.

Villa originally meant not just the *casa del padrone* – the manor house – but the whole estate with its agricultural land, *fattoria*, farm buildings, furnished with wine cellars, oil presses, fermentation and store rooms and a garden. No country house could be a villa unless it had a garden or park. In Italy a villa was so closely associated with its garden that a park without a country house was more readily regarded as a villa than a country house without a garden. North of the Alps it was different: there the villa was understood as a building to be lived in. This conceptual difference sheds light on a crucial change of direction in the development of modern garden design. In the South, house and garden were regarded as a single unit, whereas in the North the garden came to be ever more closely associated with the surrounding countryside; this was especially pronounced in the English landscape gardens of the 18th century. In Italy, villas were owned by rich patrician families and later by aristocrats, dukes, counts, as well as by cardinals and popes. They invested their fortunes equally in villas, agriculture, gardens and house. During the early Renaissance, particularly in Tuscany, the villa was still a complete unit: at the same time a centre of agricultural production and a place for spiritual and cultural renewal. The "dream of the countryside" embraced the two: agriculture and spiritual relaxation. The desire of the city dweller to own a piece of land outside the city was an ancient Mediterranean one. To grow food on one's own land, to spend a part of the summer there, had always been one of the most highly valued aspects of life. Plague in the cities lent further wing to urban-dweller visions of the joys of country life. The incipient decline of the Christian world order favoured the new role of the villa as foremost location of the longed-for Golden Age. The replacement of the monastery as the focal point of (Christian-mediaeval) culture by the villa marked the beginning of a new era. Not by chance was the villa among the cultural institutions in which the Italian Renaissance manifested itself most clearly. The most important architects of the 15th

and 16th centuries, Brunelleschi, Michelozzo, Michelangelo, Peruzzi, Bramante, Buontalenti, Vasari and Palladio, all designed villas and thus contributed to the fact that the ideals of the Renaissance were particularly exemplified in this form of architecture.

The rule of the Medici in Florence brought a powerful stimulus to secular architecture in central Italy. More peaceful times made it possible first for city palaces and later also for country houses to dispense with fortification and to be more open to the surrounding countryside. Man's sensual relationship to his environment also changed. An exaggerated, even rapturous love of the countryside is evident in many works of art of the period.

This development set garden design two new, fundamental tasks: to link the garden and house and to relate the garden to the surrounding countryside. In the Middle Ages this was not a matter for discussion: everyone wanted seclusion and protection from a hostile environment. The garden was a walled area, *hortus conclusus*, equally insulated from house and countryside. There was no attempt at architectural connection, but rather at separation, organizational clarity. The Renaissance changed this timorous and narrow view: the high walls were taken down, the

25

Garden of the *Villa il Bosco di Fonte Lucente*, Fiesole, Italy

Parterre garden with a view of Florence and the Tuscan countryside

house was made open to the garden and from the garden there were now many and diverse views of the peaceful surrounding countryside. The garden between house and countryside became the theme of the new art of garden design. From this time on, these three elements and their relationship to one another fundamentally determined the development of the garden. The relationship of these three areas within a specific set of circumstances, and the form of their interaction, are among the basic questions of garden design. In terms of the relationship between house, garden and surrounding countryside, the Villa Medici near Florence is the first true Renaissance villa. Twenty years after his return from exile Cosimo decided to create for his son Giovanni, a lover of art who was interested in the humanities, surroundings in which he could pursue his studies and enthusiasms in happy leisure on the most beautiful of the Florentine hills. The villa which he had built was no fortified country seat in extensive grounds but rather a setting for the new ideas of the Renaissance.

This Medici villa was naturally intended to announce the rebirth of the villa of classical antiquity not merely as an architectural form but also as a whole way of life and way of thinking. It was this villa, built by Michelozzo Michelozzi between 1458 and 1461 in imitation of the classical

antique style, which – in accordance with the Janus-headed character of the Renaissance – set the trend for the next two centuries of garden history.

Alberti's stipulations – that a villa should lie on the slope of a hillside close to a city with its outside walls open to the sunshine and light – were realized for the first time and in exemplary fashion in the Medici villa at Fiesole. It was wholly conceived in terms of the surrounding countryside and the climate, although its structural manipulation of the surrounding area cannot be ignored. Both house and garden were built on terraces on the sloping ground. Michelozzo's pioneering achievement was his experimentation with new transitions between house, garden and countryside. For the first time, the loggia was made a fundamental element of the villa and a central part of the garden façade, replacing the inner courtyard which had been usual up to that time and which allowed no view of the surrounding countryside. For the first time, the garden was laid out longitudinally to the building. The transition between villa and countryside takes place in rhythmic stages in the form of terraces, balustrades and staircases. Even today these garden terraces, originally decorated with geometrical flower-beds and numerous fountains, provide the most beautiful views of the surrounding countryside and of the nearby city of Florence.

Garden of the *Villa Giusti*, Verona, Italy

Agostino Giusti, a man who was as cultured as he was powerful, created this splendid villa garden in the second half of the 16th century.

Giovanni de' Medici died only two years after the completion of the gardens. Following Cosimo's death one year later, in 1464, the villa became the favourite residence of Cosimo's grandson Lorenzo and a gathering place for a circle of humanists. But new buildings soon tempted the art patron. In 1479 he bought a country estate – Poggio a Caiano. Whereas the villa in Fiesole lay within easy reach of the city, and was thus effectively a villa *suburbano*, Poggio a Caiano (Poggio means hill) lay several hours away on a small hill in the middle of a large country estate. The task facing the architect, Giuliano da Sangallo, was now quite different; the ground-plan nevertheless seems inspired by its smaller-scale predecessor, as suggested by the quadratic format, the loggia as entrance hall, the central Sala Grande and the four corner projections. In Poggio a Caiano, however, everything is more prestigious, more imposing. Approached from the Florence road, the villa first reveals its front projections. These are flanked by arcades which at one time were raised on a plinth of three steps. They offer cover from every position of the sun, disguise the farm areas, provide the building with an optical pedestal from which it looks far out across the landscape and form a broad terrace which runs right round the *piano nobile*. Today the building still stands on a regular space which is separated by walls from the surrounding garden. The corners are emphasized by tower-like pavilions. The area between the entrance portal and the villa was used for open-air receptions and parties and is therefore only planted with grass. On three sides of the building, parallel to the loggias, are geometrical flower-beds. The ornamental garden proper with its pergolas, fountains and central octagon lies, however, in no axial relationship to the building. Viewed overall, the individual elements appear to have been merely added on to one another.

The next stage of development took place just a decade later in Naples, when the Neapolitan Crown Prince Alfonso of Aragon commissioned the Florentine architect Giuliano da Maiano with the design of two summer residences. Both the smaller La Ducchesca and the legendary Poggio Reale contained magnificent gardens, now long since destroyed.

Poggio Reale was designed for summer recreation, and the Mediterranean climate of the Gulf of Naples made it possible to linger in the open air until late at night. The palace was a matchless setting for the magnificent banquets held by the Neapolitan kings and viceroys, Charles VIII and Juan d'Austria. Plays were staged at the garden parties and poets such as Pontano and Giuliano de Scorciatis recited from their works. In the centre of the building lay an ornamental inner courtyard, three steps lower than the building, forming a kind of rectangular amphitheatre. This open-air theatre was also the villa's banqueting hall. At a nod from Alfonso, countless jets of water would spray out of the ground, soaking the dining guests until at last the entire area was flooded. Precedents for this sunken amphitheatre were to be found in the palaces of antiquity and the Alhambra.

Thanks to the careful research of art historian Christoph Luitpold Frommel, we are now able to form an impression of the lost gardens. Here, too, the solution offered to the problem of transition between house and garden was to prove crucial to garden evolution. Leaving the palace by the rear portal one found oneself in an open anteroom bordered on its sides by two loggias each with five axes.

In the centre was a pool whose water was supplied from the garden lying behind and above it. Behind the pool a little stairway led up to this higher terraced garden. This terrace was surrounded on all sides by walls into which were set niches containing statues. In the middle of an arbour of bitter orange trees which lay on the right was a further loggia with ornamental arcades and a balcony which jutted out over a similarly rectangular fishpond which lay below. A row of trees on the opposite bank completed the geometrical design of the garden.

Adjoining the palace were further flower-beds, while behind there must have been an open-air *corso* for horse-racing, recalling the hippodromes of ancient Greece and Rome. Besides these strictly geometrical complexes, which together made up a long rectangle, there were extensive orchards of olive, fig, pear, date, apple and pomegranate trees, laurel and orange groves, vineyards with the most exquisite grapes, herb gardens with rosemary, marjoram and sage plants, a rose garden and finally animal enclosures and a spacious hunting park. Alfonso had continuously and unscrupulously expropriated land from his neighbours in order to extend his property and, by the time of his overthrow in 1494, the grounds reached as far as the sea.

There is a clear connection between Poggio a Caiano and Poggio Reale: each is a variation of the same type, namely the Renaissance villa derived from the four-turreted castle. Whereas a city palace was usually bound by the proportions and alignments of the buildings which already existed in its street, a country residence could assert itself freely and without restraints in the open countryside. The pronounced projections in the villa architecture thus fulfilled two functions: they imparted a new corporeality to the façades and thus complemented the setting of the villa on its hilly slope, visible from a long distance off. The new esteem in which the countryside was held found in villa architecture in general an appropriate means of expression. In place of insulation and fortification, the new precepts of architecture were openness and adaptation. But the protruding corner bays not only gave the building a more three-dimensional appearance, they also framed the view. The same, new relationship of the building to its environment, as demonstrated by the project bays at Poggio Reale, can also be observed in the grounds. The longitudinal axis became the determining factor in the transition between indoors and outdoors. It represented a first step towards spatial continuity and led ultimately to the conception of house and garden as a single unit.

In only fifty years, architecture in Florence had completed the transition from the mediaeval castle to the mature villa. In Rome, architectural development was less consistent and more influenced by external factors. But building nevertheless received a tremendous impetus there, too, as countless artists from Florence, among them Alberti, Michelangelo und Vasari, came to Rome to work. Following the return of the popes from Avignon, Rome became more and more a centre of innovation. Bramante's Belvedere courtyard in the Vatican, begun in 1503, in many ways represents a summary of the architectural achievements of the previous century. Its linking of a longitudinal theatre courtyard, surrounded by loggia, with a higher-level ornamental garden is directly related to Poggio Reale. The connecting function of the longitudinal axis dominates the Belvedere courtyard. What developed from the needs of the country house manifested itself in Rome as an independent and monumental architecture of open spaces.

The garden as a landscape of ideas
by Torsten Olaf Enge

I. Taking leave of Paradise

History is like an enormous, overgrown wood. If the observer, the wanderer, the friend of nature is not simply to lose himself in a thick jungle of undergrowth and a sheer impenetrable confusion of seemingly quite arbitrary coincidences he requires all the strength and will of a cultivated mind. Pathways, avenues and lanes must be laid, clearings and open spaces made and once everything has been well ordered, everything else, if possible general, comprehensive perspectives opened up. There have always been gardens – created by Semiramis, the Greeks, in the Middle Ages, right up to the modern age. History does not suggest that all at once during the Renaissance and the Baroque period something quite new happened. In history there is always a before and an after. That a new idea can suddenly come into being and alter reality, in a way which – despite influences and borrowings – is nevertheless innovative, is as significant for the wood (apprehensive about its natural state) as it is for history with its concern for continuity. But there's no help for it. If we wish to stroll in the garden of the past, then the wood will have to lose trees. Possibly a great many, including some of the finest specimens.

Small temple in the garden of the *Trianon* Versailles, France

A starting-point such as this may strike some contemporary readers as the highest form of rationalist brutality. In an age when the tree as such is virtually sacred, interfering with nature seems almost criminal, only justifiable in so far as it helps nature to achieve with greater intensity, with greater purity, its true essence, which is understood as a state opposing human planning and intervention and living for and from itself. The chopping down of healthy trees, the trimming and training of hedges and bushes into artificial shapes in the name of art, viewed in these terms, seems a virtually incomprehensible mental aberration. How, then, is it still possible to wander through a baroque garden today without feeling both distress and repugnance at one and the same time?

There are two ways. The first is the most obvious and most often chosen: one appropriates from the past only those aspects which are still valid in the present and one enjoys only those parts of nature which, even in their most distorted manifestations, match one's expectations: the brilliant display of flowers in the ornamental flower-beds, the contrast of colours, the splendid trees, the long walks in the fresh air and the distance from the city. Thus the landscape gardens of the 17th and 18th centuries have become public parks in which subjectivity, seeking release, attempts to break free from the constraints of a civilization dominated by technology. Thanks to its underlying bourgeois structure, this subjectivity succeeds in accommodating the rigorous severity of Baroque parks within its own sense of order. True admiration first makes an appearance in the case of English gardens, however, in which the illusion of naturalness allows one to overlook the calculated nature of the arrangement and where one can in good conscience surrender to a sensation of naturalness. But we are

Hermitage Bayreuth, Germany
Avenue of trees

only truly at home in the larger sections of wood, far removed from views and perspectives. There contemporary man feels himself cocooned in confusion. He feels unobserved and – in the face of a vegetation which behaves indifferently towards him – allowed to be himself.

The second way is less direct. It does not attempt to circumvent history, but at the same time is not prepared to trace the substance of ideas purely to their historical contingency. These two premises are, however, virtually incompatible. Their contradiction lies in their attempt to acknowledge a point in the past while nevertheless remaining a-historical. But history cannot be dismissed so easily. Nor is this our aim. The naivety of the first way lies in its assumption that the gardens of the Renaissance and Baroque are within easy reach. This certainty comes from the conviction that a wood remains a wood, regardless of time or place. Such tautologies are to be mistrusted, however, since they only seemingly free themselves from temporality, while failing to notice that, in the context of such an alleged universality, the idea of their own presence is lost. "A-historic" does not mean "indeterminate". Ideas are neither generalized empty formulae nor fine-sounding clichés but concrete forms of being which must be very precisely defined and distinguished from one another. And thus the first revelation of the second way is this: a wood is *not* a wood, a tree is *not* a tree, nature is *not* an eternal incarnation of self-perpetuating objectivity standing in perpetual opposition to the subject.

It is thus initially a negation which halts the unthinking consumption of the past. And yet this important, seemingly so simple step does not necessarily save us from absorbing ourselves in merely "historical observations". To localize the point of origin of an idea, it is necessary to overcome such formal considerations, put ourselves on the level of ideas themselves and test these ideas one against the other. Determining the origins of the Renaissance garden requires a dual approach, as in geometry. A point on a straight line can be reached from two directions. In our case the straight line is the linearity of time, history. But in the same way that the point is never a part of the straight line, so the idea is never part of history. One idea can only be defined by another idea; it thereby becomes "clear", "comprehensible". But it is only through the differentiation of two of its sides on the temporal line that an idea acquires its a-historical-chronological dimension.

The title "Taking leave of Paradise" is an attempt to indicate this dual approach, which is not just historical, looking back to the past, but equally considers the present. Only thus does the a-historical nature of the idea come into view. One of the many possible images of paradise in the present day has already been hinted at above. This is the "wood", the "park", the "countryside" as the *ideational location* for subjective recreation: in a word, *nature*. Photography is perhaps the most appropriate medium through which to express these images, since it is concerned less with the actual existence than with the imagining of Paradise. The power of the imagination does not require real examples in order to become active. It is satisfied with selective stimulants, as long as these are manifoldly "promising". Photography does this better than any modern painting since it can unite such ideational concepts as sun, greenness, freedom and naturalness so realistically within one picture.

Besides this aesthetic side, which imagines Paradise as a general state of well-being, the – ever bourgeois – present also allows itself an ideality of individuality in which it can view not only nature but also itself as realized in detail. This is the "garden" in its dual function as both ornamental and useful. The ideational "person" in bourgeois society is not the individual but rather the family (see Hegel's Philosophy of Law §§ 158 ff.). Thus the "house", surrounded by a "garden", is first and foremost the house of the family and serves to portray a complex unit. This self-realization has two sides. The first is external sociability: the garden must represent, compete, assert its specialness, but at the same time fit in, communicate with other gardens while nevertheless functioning as a protective zone. The other side is less visible. It usually takes place behind the house: the useful side of the garden, the planting of vegetables and herbs, the building of greenhouses for the well-being and upkeep of the family.

"Garden", "park" and "wood" are thus synonymous in our times with the ideals of beauty, naturalness and health. It is advisable to familiarize oneself in as much detail as possible with their ideational imaginative power if one wishes to approach the ideas of garden and countryside in the Renaissance and Baroque in their absoluteness.

The pictures of "Paradise" as visualized by the late Middle Ages refer to quite different fields. Their origin is clearly the Old Testament Garden of Eden. Eden represents a universal variable which can be applied to all ages. For the 14th and 15th centuries right up to Michelangelo, however, there exists an even more powerful illustration of a typical ideal garden landscape: the Earthly Paradise which Dante described in his *Divine Comedy* in the 27th Canto of Purgatory. As soon as the poet, climbing up towards heaven, enters this holy garden, the worlds part. Virgil, who has been his companion up until this point, now leaves him, because someone who has reached thus far has achieved freedom in both the physical and the spiritual sense and mastery of himself. He no longer has need of an emperor or pope, nor of a classical poet to make his decisions for him. As a symbol of Dante's autonomy, Virgil sets upon his head both a crown and a mitre:

> Non aspettar mio dir più né mio cenno:
> libero, dritto e sano è tuo arbitrio,
> e fallo fora non fare a suo senno;
> perch'io te sopra te corono e mitrio.

The circles of hell have at last been conquered. The body has been completely cleansed of its sins of arrogance, envy, gluttony and lust. The Earthly Paradise has become a garden of purified and exalted existence: a place for the elect few, those chosen by divine Providence. It is easy to see the ideality of this *locus amoenus*. It is more difficult not to overlook the "naturalness" of this paradisaical garden. Dante makes no attempt to describe a distant world of the hereafter, but places his words firmly within the context of nature:

> Eager already to search in and round
> The heavenly forest, dense and living-green,
> Which tempered to the eyes the new-born day,
> Withouten more delay I left the bank,
> Taking the level country slowly, slowly
> Over the soil that everywhere breathes fragrance.
> A softly-breathing air, that no mutation

Had in itself upon the forehead smote me
No heavier blow than that of a gentle wind,
Whereat the branches, lightly tremulous,
Did all of them bow downward toward that side
Where its first shadow casts the Holy Mountain;
Yet not from their upright direction swayed,
So that the little birds upon their tops
Should leave the practice of each art of theirs;
(*Purgatory*, 28th Canto, from the translation by H. W. Longfellow)

Garden of the *Villa Garzoni*, Collodi, Italy
View of the maze

The wood, the rustle of leaves, the chirping of birds, a mild wind and shady spots set the scene. Two rivers flow through it, the *Lethe* and the *Eunoia*. In the one, Lethe, everything is forgotten that belongs to the past and that is unsuitable for life in the garden. In the other, the newcomer gains the true way of thinking which is oriented solely to good. This paradisaical garden also has a central house, one which gives everything both its status and its significance: the *church* in its symbolic and highest secular form as a triumphal carriage, moving forward, unstoppable. The inhabitants of this Earthly Paradise were portrayed many times in the art of the 14th and 15th centuries. They appear first and foremost as the Holy Family, often including Saint Anne and John the Baptist as a boy, followed by other saints and finally outstanding individuals: members of the nobility,

34

Garden of the *Villa Aldobrandini,*
Frascati, Italy
Ornamental garden with view of the villa

merchants, patrons of the arts. The countryside in the background re-
sembles, more and more successfully, Tuscany or Umbria and yet at the
same time manages to transform these familiar settings into places of
absolute perfection, designed according to strict principles. The result is
an "idealized naturalness". This has frequently been viewed as the break
with the Middle Ages and the beginning of the modern age. But we should
not be deceived. Nature as portrayed up to the times of Perugino, Raphael
and Leonardo lacks any form of immediacy or independence. It remains
a divine creation, which only the chosen deserve to inhabit. The garden
as idealized landscape is a hierarchical construct to which only the *indi-*
vidual who is on a never-ending journey gains admittance, as for instance
Dante seeking Beatrice. It is not difficult to see Raphael's Vatican frescoes
as a faithful illustration of the *Divine Comedy.* It is thus only logical that
Raphael not only transports Dante to Mount Parnassus, but also integrates
him into his *Disputa.* For these describe the framework from which derives
the justification for the selective purification processes which ordain the
sacred Mount of the Muses and the School of Athens as the summits of
a celestially elite cosmic order.

The idea of the Italian garden in the palaces and villas of the 15th century
can be interpreted in a very similar fashion. Such gardens represented
highly-cultivated places of refuge based on education and intellectual
selection, on cultivation and an elite view of man, in which much of the
world was left behind and where man's inner essence was prepared for a

higher existence. The Medici family and its Florentine Academy are characteristic phenomena of this last phase of the Middle Ages.

The real break was made by Brunelleschi and took place in pure architecture rather than in any of the applied arts such as garden design. Painting only followed much later. Nor can Alberti be seen as an innovator as regards the idea of the garden. The few remarks which he made about the design of gardens in his theoretical work *Ten Books on Architecture* remain anchored in the Middle Ages and make few advances beyond Pliny or other models from classical antiquity. Looking back to antiquity is not in itself a sign of a new beginning.

The structure of the *Divine Comedy* would fall apart without the intellectual horizon of ancient Rome, its history, its literature and, unexpectedly in such a Christian work, Roman mythology.

It was Bramante who first succeeded in applying the new impetus to garden architecture. His masterpiece, the Belvedere courtyard, was greatly praised by his contemporaries. Unfortunately very little of it has been preserved. If one examines the old drawings and engravings it is hard to understand why this particular *cortile* had so much effect on the development of garden design.

Bramante's achievement, which earned not only praise but also much criticism, can only be truly measured when one compares the Belvedere courtyard with his parallel rebuilding of St. Peter's. In 1503 he began work on the courtyard complex, in 1506 on the new building of the basilica. He was unable to finish either of these projects, since he died in 1514. But his plans, and the works already executed, proved of lasting influence. In the middle of the 15th century Pope Nicholas V had been the first to take in hand the modernization and partial restoration of the old, five-aisled church building which dated back to the 4th century. Fifty years after Nicholas' death, Pope Julius II again took up the plan, but ordered a completely new building in which the mausoleum which he had commissioned from Michelangelo would have a central place. Bramante's decision to demolish the original building along with all its altars, tombs and pillars when it was not strictly necessary was denounced by many, including Michelangelo himself, as a barbaric act. By the time Luther visited Rome in 1512 only a few vestiges remained of the original venerable building, irrelevant trifles compared to the immense piers of the new building already erected.

In common with all large basilicas, the old St. Peter's had an atrium in front of its entrance portal, a kind of forecourt or garden with a fountain where churchgoers could meet and wash themselves before entering the church. The atrium, with its multiple functions, preserved a central idea of the mediaeval garden as the approach area to the house of God. In his plans for the new building, Bramante explicitly chose not to follow this model and thus to depart from the traditional relationship between garden and place of worship. The ground plan of St. Peter's was conceived as a Greek cross, without atrium, without nave, flooded with light, with all its parts given equal emphasis and with a large public square on the entrance side. Bramante freed the idea of the garden from the church and transferred it to the pope's secular, private sphere. It is only in this context that the originality of the Belvedere becomes clear. The sacred and the profane go their separate ways. The garden is no longer the area leading to a higher existence on the other side, in the way that the Earthly Paradise as depicted by Dante was the preliminary stage leading to a Heavenly Paradise. The Belvedere is in itself an expression of the highest form of existence. The traveller is not invited to pass quickly through, but to linger in what is now itself a perfect place.

The dimension essential to fulfil this new role is art and art alone, and one which is no longer tied to the church and thus to religion. Julius II had deposited his extensive collection of ancient and modern sculptures in the Belvedere villa. By deliberately linking this villa to the Pope's private palace via the *cortile*, Bramante created – with the aid of art – a counter-

Belvedere, Rome, Italy
Engraving by Stefano Pera

balance to the directly adjacent church area which effectively placed the Pope as individual and ruler within a living space independent of religion. Contemporary observers clearly recognized this fact. It led ultimately to fierce criticism of the courtyard and to its subsequent disfigurement, which was intended to put an end to an all too worldly concept.

This "dimension of art" means more than merely the art collection in the villa. Similar collections of antiques had existed before. Much more crucial is the architectural design of the courtyard itself, which expresses an entirely independent power. Bramante enclosed the courtyard within a multi-storeyed system of arcades and loggias, thus making the garden an independent, self-contained unit. Bramante emphasized the introspective aspect of his design by ensuring that all sides of the courtyard, and in particular the amphitheatre on the palace side and the loggia of the exedra opposite, turned the attention to the garden – and never beyond. This self-containing unit remained prototypical for Italian gardens throughout the 16th century, despite occasional divergences from its original purity. The simple perfection of the Belvedere courtyard appeared to many historians to be a revival of Roman tradition. No one would dispute the influence of the shrine of Fortuna or the hippodrome architecture of Roman times. But in no building of classical antiquity can be found this entirely modern, concrete expression of individual unity.

This thesis only becomes comprehensible when one looks at the most important achievement of the Belvedere courtyard, that which differentiates it from all the mere imitations of classical models: the interior division of the grounds as a whole into three parts, namely a spacious area for festivals and tournaments, a central terrace and a further spacious area in front of the villa. This is not simply a matter of purely formal structure. Bramante assigned a quite definite content to each level: to the upper, "art"; to the lower, "artistry". The terrace between the two could claim no individual characteristic content but rather was there to signal the fact that the fields of art and sport do not merge directly into one another but rather require some form of mediation. To mediate means not just to connect, it can also mean to divide and to keep separate. This was the dual task of the middle level. If we examine this order in philosophical terms we see the real meaning of the three-tiered terrace garden:

1. *Mind* (here in the form of art) and *body* (physis as the world of sporting events and festivals) do not form a unity. They are parts of a comprehensive whole but do not blend into amorphous indistinction.

2. Mind and body are not equal. The mind is ranked above the body. This was the decision of the modern age. Bramante here in no way fell back on hierarchies of the past. Body and mind are separated from each other as pure disjunction, beyond which lie no further levels. The question of domination is one of principle not of order.

3. There is a process of mediation between mind and body which constitutes its own level of reality. Bramante expressed this process architecturally in his use of stairways. A large flight of steps led from the sports ground up to the middle level. From here, a massive ramp divided into two parts led up to the level of art. Physical momentum may be sufficient to reach the first level. To attain further heights, it must employ the help of other sources of energy. Bramante here also reintroduces an important element of the basilica atrium, now freed from its sacred setting and used in a highly profane form: the *fountain* and *water*. In gardens of modern history, water does not serve to cleanse and prepare for an ultimately transcendental act; rather, it represents – in accordance with its ideational content – the internal, indeed the personality-immanent process which unites body and mind into one. The person striving upwards to the level of art first met water in the fountain in the central niche of the ramp. Should he decide to continue on his way, he was accompanied by water in the form of small fountains set into the retaining walls of the ramp. He is thus already half-way there. But Bramante knew that the principle of the power of purification from the physical was to be found not in the process itself (architecturally speaking, not in the water itself) but in the mind. He therefore placed a large, free-standing fountain in the very centre of the topmost level. There, water itself became matter. Collected in a heavy bowl, it cleared the way to the real goal: the beauties of the Belvedere.

The first garden of the modern age has nothing more in common with Dante's Earthy Paradise. There is no rustling of trees, no chirping of birds, no flowing Lethe and no waiting Beatrice. The church has been resolutely excluded from the garden. The garden is instead ruled by art and by a pope highly interested in secular power. No pathway leads from here up to heavenly spheres. All coming and going takes place purely within the garden, in a process which is always identical, regardless of whether performed by Julius II, Machiavelli or indeed any other visitor.

Garden of the *Villa il Bosco di Fonte Lucente*, Fiesole, Italy

ILLUSTRATION ON PAGE 40:
Entrance to the mirror grotto and the Great Mask in the garden of the Villa Giusti Verona, Italy

38

Renaissance and Mannerist Gardens

Gardens of the
VILLA D'ESTE
Tivoli · Italy

Appointed Governor of Tivoli following his failure to win the papal elections, Cardinal Ippolito d'Este began, in 1550, the rebuilding of his seat of government. The former Benedictine cloister was not splendid enough for the son of Lucretia Borgia, and so he commissioned the Renaissance artist Pirro Ligorio with its renovation. The plans, in which the garden was envisaged as a complementary and integral part of the house, were based on an architectural design conforming substantially to the laws of geometry and perspective.

The garden is clearly divided into three parts: one lower, on level ground, and two rising in terraces towards the villa. Its basic form, which is repeated in many of its details, is the square.

The execution of the project caused the architect G. Alberto Galvani more than minor difficulties: one whole district of Tivoli had to be demolished in order to clear enough space for the grounds. In addition, the garden, which for climatic reasons was to be north-facing, had to be underpinned to a quite considerable extent because the mountain range on which it lay ran north-west. Originally, in contrast to the present day, the garden was entered not from above, through the villa, but through an entrance gate bordered by two fountains on the lower level. From an old engraving one can see that there were originally arbours by the gate and also an amphitheatre with statues symbolizing the liberal arts. Their exposed position ensured that the visitor was attuned right from the very beginning of his walk up to the villa, to the outlook on life and intellectual stance of its owner, a true Renaissance nobleman.

Pergolas laid out in the form of a cross divided the level region, which one entered first, into four equal squares. There were small pavilions from

Avenue of the Hundred Fountains
Engraving by Venturini

which the visitor could observe the flower and herb borders. At their intersection, where a wooden summer-house originally stood, there is now a rotunda with what are probably the oldest cypresses in Italy. This complex was to have been bordered laterally by two mazes of evergreen hedgerows on each side; in the end, only the south-west ones were

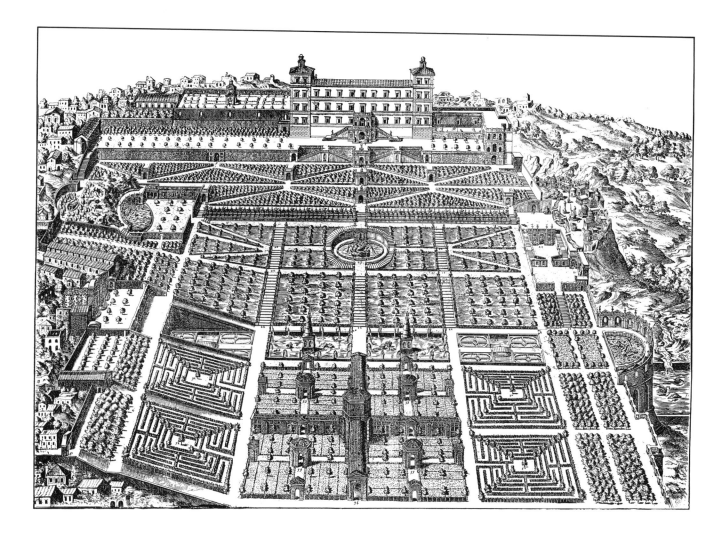

completed. This lower region was bounded by rows of trees on its outside edges, and by fishponds on the side facing the villa. Four ponds were planned but only three built. On the side overlooking the valley, an exedra-shaped panoramic terrace – only existing in the plans – was to have emphasized this first lateral axis, which separates the lower from the upper garden. This design feature is reinforced on the opposite, ascending slope of the garden by the celebrated "water organ". This organ functioned purely mechanically: air, compressed by the cascading waters, caused the pipes of the artfully constructed organ to sound, and set figures in motion.

Its pendant, also on the hilly side of the garden but somewhat nearer to the villa, was a fountain decorated with owls and other birds. The pathway to the villa continues via three parallel flights of steps on two levels, decorated by cascading waterfalls. On the second level the middle flight of steps divides to embrace the oval basin of the Dragon fountain, which was planned as the iconological centre of the garden. The second main lateral axis is formed by the Avenue of the Hundred Fountains, almost 150 metres long, where water pours from stone obelisks, eagles, little boats and lillies into a trough-shaped channel, and then spouts through chimera heads into a second, lower channel. The Ovato fountains – an artificial rock massif of grottoes and allegorical sculptures – and the Rometta fountains – a miniature reproduction of ancient Rome – are two further interesting stopping-points on the way to the villa.

The impressive garden of the Villa d'Este is distinctly different from the villa gardens of Tuscany.

ABOVE:
Ovato Fountain

OPPOSITE:
Fountain of Nature

FOLLOWING DOUBLE PAGE:
The Dragon or Wheel of Fire Fountain

OPPOSITE PAGE:
Neptune Fountain and Water Organ

RIGHT:
Chimera head from the Avenue of the
Hundred Fountains

BELOW:
Avenue of the Hundred Fountains

Gardens of the
PALAZZINA FARNESE
Caprarola · Italy

Giacomo Barozzi da Vignola – after Michelangelo's death, the leading architect in Rome – began in about 1540 with the construction of the family seat of Cardinal Alessandro II Farnese, which lay not far from Bomarzo at the edge of the little town of Caprarola near Viterbo. It was Vignola's first major work and it is probable that he also designed the garden. The estate lay long forgotten, and was only recently restored – in an unobtrusive and economical manner which allows the visitor to trace even now the patina of the past.

The fortress-style villa, a pentagon with projecting cornices, was closely flanked by two high-walled parterre gardens forming the two arms of the letter Y. The parterres lay at the same level as the first floor of the villa and could only be reached from the villa via two bridges. Their main axis terminated in a number of grottoes, and they were separated from the house by a deep moat. Today, however, not much remains of these parterres laid out in mediaeval style, nor of the fruit orchards enclosed by high box and the interweaving vaulted pergolas in the middle of which a fountain played.

The garden, well worth a visit even today, is part of the Palazzina, a sort of intimate private residence, which the Cardinal of Farnese had built above the Palazzo and where he could find peace and quiet. The Palazzina, with its own little park, forms an independent architectural unit and can be reached from the villa through a now completely overgrown grove of

The exedra-shaped boundary of the garden

majestic sweet chestnut trees, cedars and pines. These tall, mature trees give place to a square lawn containing a circular pool from which a fountain spouts.

Between the side walls of two coarsely-textured, very solid-looking grotto tunnels, a broad staircase leads up to the casino. It is divided down the middle by a small waterfall which is edged by interlinking stone elements.

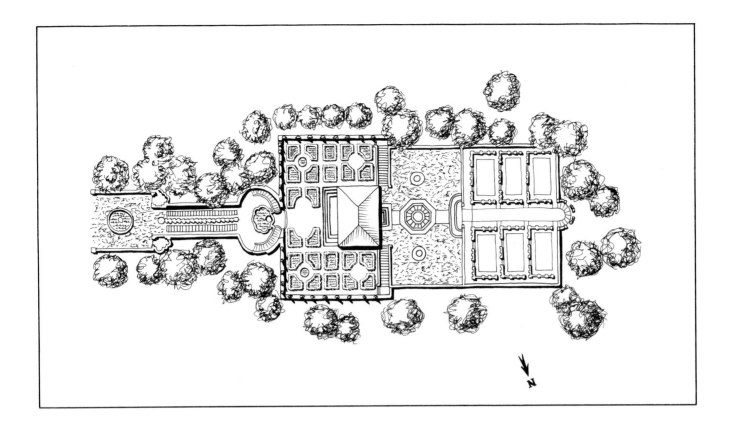

The stairs lead up to a wonderfully harmonious, oval garden which ends in a large, scalloped pool. Its waters are supplied from a huge, overflowing stone chalice. To the right and left recline two monumental river gods with weighty cornucopias, who support themselves on the chalice's rim. Viewed from below, they seem not only to watch over the fountain but also to protect the house. Two broad, gently ascending staircases, one on each side, lead the visitor to the parterre garden proper. A low wall surrounds this ornamental garden on three sides. It delimits the terraced garden and simultaneously serves as a bench. Vase-carrying herms and caryatids, lively and expressive garden gods and goddesses, adorn the wall every few metres. Each of the 28 statues is different. Within this enclosure, box hedges line symmetrical flower-beds which, together with the two hippopotamus fountains at their centre, enliven the scene.

Next to the Palazzina, two broad flights of stairs, lined with waterfalls cascading from dolphins to basins in turn, lead up to the highest terrace, which lies behind the house.

At the foot of the stairway the water pours into a scalloped bowl and then flows into a round pool. In the middle of the square, a circular basin with a fountain is surrounded by a beautiful and intricate octagonal pebble-stone mosaic. A gently sloping path, edged by a little wall which rises in three steps, leads up to four oversize stone monuments in the front of which are high, semi-circular niches and a sort of protruding seat. The monuments are arranged in exedra shape and are decorated with stone busts, sculptures and amphorae. They conclude the flower parterre, originally laid out in three terraces and now completely overgrown by grass, against the picturesque backdrop of the wood.

FOLLOWING DOUBLE PAGE:
Fountain with river gods in front of the
Palazzina Farnese

ABOVE AND OPPOSITE PAGE:
Boundary walls of the parterre garden with
herms and caryatids

Gardens of the
VILLA GAMBERAIA
Settignano · Italy

On the site of the Villa Gamberaia, on the outskirts of Settignano to the east of Florence, there stood in the 14th century a simple farmhouse owned by nuns. The house changed hands twice more before being bought in 1618 by the rich merchant Zanobi Lapi. Lapi had a park landscaped and, while remaining true to the house's basic form, rebuilt it as a typical Florentine villa, with clean, harmonious lines.

One hundred years later the wealthy Capponi family took over the property. The family made few changes to the house but enlarged the garden considerably, effectively giving it the form it has today.

During the Second World War, all but the outer walls of the house burnt down. The garden, too, was damaged almost beyond recognition. It was only reconstructed in 1954 by Marcello Marchi. The laborious restoration work on the basis of old and drawings took six years to complete. The house's present owner has made only a few changes to the reconstructed gardens; it was he who planted, between the boxtrees, the luxuriant roses whose blooms provide a counterpoint of colour and form to their neighbouring hedges.

The approach to the house is a little to one side and leads to the architecturally unostentatious narrow side of the house. Behind the building, on the south side, is an impressive parterre. Originally an orchard of fruit trees blossomed here; as a ground plan dating from the 17th century reveals, however, these had to make way for a *parterre de broderies*. The garden was given its final form – still viewable today – at the end of the last century by the then owner, the Rumanian Princess Giovanna Ghyka. Carefully-clipped boxtrees line the paths, stone benches invite the visitor to rest, while fine pebble mosaics, rose-bushes, lemon trees in terracotta

Balustrade ornamented with statues

pots and four elongated pools created by the princess give the garden its peaceful, luxurious charm. At the end of this area is a semicircular waterlily pond, behind which an exedra-shaped cypress hedge screens the garden at the top end from the hilly olive groves. Carefully-trimmed archways – created by the present owners – offer marvellous views of the Tuscan countryside.

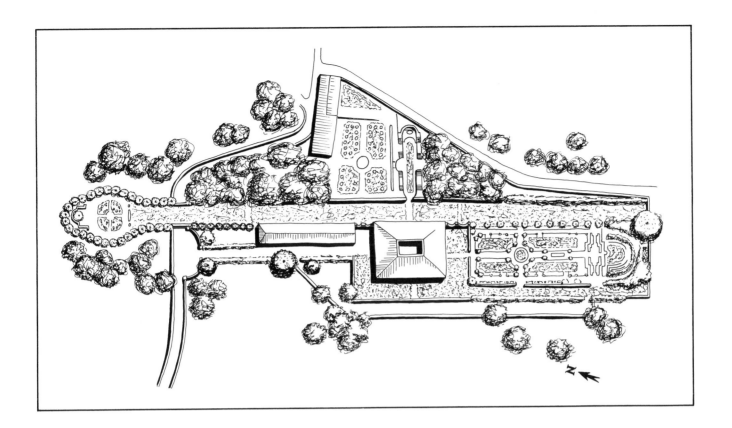

Parallel to the villa and to this part of the garden runs a grass avenue, almost 10 metres wide and 30 metres long, which measures the entire length of the garden and terminates in a terrace at the top end. From here there is also a good view of the olive plantations and vineyards which surround the Villa Gamberaia like a country estate.

The "prato", once lined by dark and towering cypresses, is flanked on one side by the villa and on the other by a high retaining wall. The wall is decorated with many different figures which rhythmically accentuate the transition from the dark shadiness of the woods and the grottoes to the sunlit terrace and the open Tuscan countryside. A small opening allows access to a separate little garden cut into the hillside, a variation on the nymphaeum theme. Pebble mosaics, an extravagant abundance of sandstone and terracotta figures and a sea of dazzling blooms from spring through to late summer turn this secluded spot, cooled by a massive fountain, into a small paradise. A double stairway leads on one side up to a bosket of holm oaks and on the other to the orangery; here, in addition to the cultivation of orange and lemon trees, summer plants were raised, cuttings set and herbs grown. The *prato* passes by a second holm oak grove and comes to an almost oval grotto garden ringed by cypress trees, with a mighty figure of Neptune at the end.

Their intelligent design gives the grounds of la Gamberaia a lucidity which in turn contributes to their intimate character.

The balance of light and shadow, the restricted use of stylistic devices and the simplicity of the geometrical rules and perspective principles which determine its composition make it a true gem among Tuscan gardens.

The Villa Gamberaia viewed from the garden

Grotto garden

OPPOSITE PAGE:
Grotto with fountain and cypresses

Gardens of the
VILLA ALDOBRANDINI
Frascati · Italy

Around 1600 Cardinal Pietro Aldobrandini commissioned the architect Giacomo della Porta, a pupil of Michelangelo, with the design of his summer residence. In a period where garden architecture was advancing alongside ecclesiastical architecture to the forefront of the arts, not only were estates growing in scale but gardens were becoming increasingly lavish and Baroque in their design. The decorations which embellish interiors to the point of gaudiness fuse outdoors, integrated into the setting of an expansive landscape, into a unique composition.

Approaching from the direction of Rome, one can see the villa from a long distance away. The width of the house, more than four times greater than its depth, is especially eye-catching. In order to make optimum use of the available space – essential in view of the utility rooms and staff quarters which a sojourn in the country naturally also necessitated – the magnificent terraces in front of and to the sides of the building were fully extended. As inconspicuously as possible, however, since nothing could be allowed to interfere with the overall impression of beauty. The kitchen chimneys, for instance, were placed at the end of the side terraces and disguised as small ornamental towers. This principle applied not only to the design of the buildings, but also to economic cultivation. Agricultural areas were enclosed within tall, decoratively trimmed hedges, so that the cornfields, vegetable beds and small vineyards were invisible to the visitor. In addition, all the avenues are copiously adorned with statues, fountains and other decorations, so that the visitor can easily imagine himself to be in a park designed purely for enjoyment. A wall with a wrought-iron

Boat fountain
Engraving by Falda

gate separates this piece of land from the actual garden area. Nowadays the entrance, as in many other villas, is up at the house. Originally, however, it was placed so that one had a view of the villa all the way up. It stands about half-way up the grounds, which scale the Frascati hillside.

Originally, after passing through the gate, one walked through an avenue of holm oaks, flanked on both sides by dense, regularly trimmed pergolas, towards a fountain decorated with beautiful mosaics. Near the middle

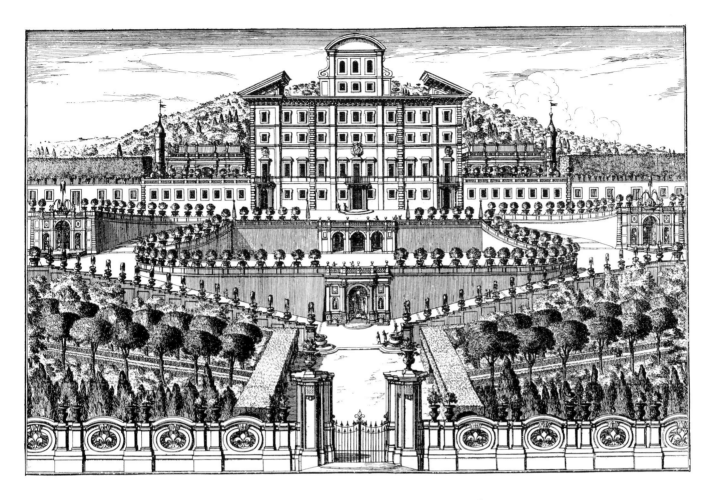

Idealized front view
Engraving by Specchi

path, two diagonal, hedge-lined avenues of pines traverse the *podere*. From the fountain, two gently-sloping paths curve up to the first terrace. Their stone banisters are topped by orange and lemon trees, and little grottoes with waterworks are set into the retaining walls. A further pair of staircases, leading to the second terrace and the entrance portal to the villa, completes the lines of an ellipse which runs at right angles to the longitudinal axis of the garden. Of the ornamental parterre gardens originally laid out at the side of the building only one, rather poorly preserved example remains. In their place today stand magnificent old plane trees in circular beds of hydrangeas surrounded by shrub grasses.

Behind the villa, a few steps lead up a generous open space – the geometrical pendant to the stairs at the front – which ends in a water theatre cut into the hillside. Here, too, the wall is decorated. Pilasters divide it into five grotto-like niches in each of which mechanical waterworks depict scenes from mythology. The main fountain in the middle shows Atlas carrying the world on his shoulders. Countless jets of water spray out of this globe and foam over moss-covered rocks into a large, semicircular basin. A staircase, water cascading down it, which leads up the slope behind this *teatro delle acque*, is visually accentuated by a wood of mighty holm oaks. The stairway leads to two high pillars from each of which a water jet gushes and then winds, garland-like, round the pillars before pouring down the stairs.

Waterworks accompany the pathway leading up to a small plateau on which stands the *Fontana dei pastori* with two figures of peasants or shepherds. The pathway then continues up to the final terrace with its *Fontana rustica*, a natural tuff grotto. A high hedge, left in its natural state, separates it from the surrounding forest.

FOLLOWING DOUBLE PAGES:
Semicircular water theatre and detailed views

Gardens of the
VILLA GARZONI
Collodi · Italy

At the beginning of the 17th century Romano Garzoni commissioned the humanist-educated patrician Ottaviano Diodati from Lucca with the most prestigious possible decoration of his house and garden. Within a few years Francesco Sbarra was able to describe the terraces and generously laid-out semicircular entrance to the villa. The many fountains and water-works were added almost a hundred years later by one of Romano Garzoni's grandsons according to Diodati's plans, giving the garden the form which can still be admired today.

The estate, which is close to Collodi, is a novel combination of a pastoral "Luccan" interpretation of the Florentine Renaissance with the emerging Baroque style. Clear forms and simple proportions, a legacy from the classical world, dominate the ground-plan of the garden, which is in bloom virtually the whole year round. But the elaboration of its features and many of its details are decidedly ornate, and illustrate a clearly Mannerist quality.

The garden welcomes its visitors with a broad, gloriously colourful parterre. Waterlilies float and swans glide upon two circular pools, from which jets of water soar to a height of almost ten metres. The pools are located in the first half of the parterre and are surrounded by flower-beds; these are no longer severely geometrical in contour, but instead create ornamental contrasts of colour, form and fragrance with flowers and box hedges. A French influence is clearly recognizable here.

Overall view of the lower part
of the garden,
seen from the steps

At the entrance, the visitor is met by the goddess Flora and Pan playing his pipes. Diana and Apollo now send him on his way into the second part of the garden, which rises imperceptibly uphill. The proud owner has made his presence felt in this part of the garden, whose box hedges and coloured stone mosaics arranged in the form of the Garzoni coat of arms and the Garzoni family initials. The box hedges which enclose the parterre are trimmed into a topiary of fantasy animals, placing ornamental accents in this front part of the garden.

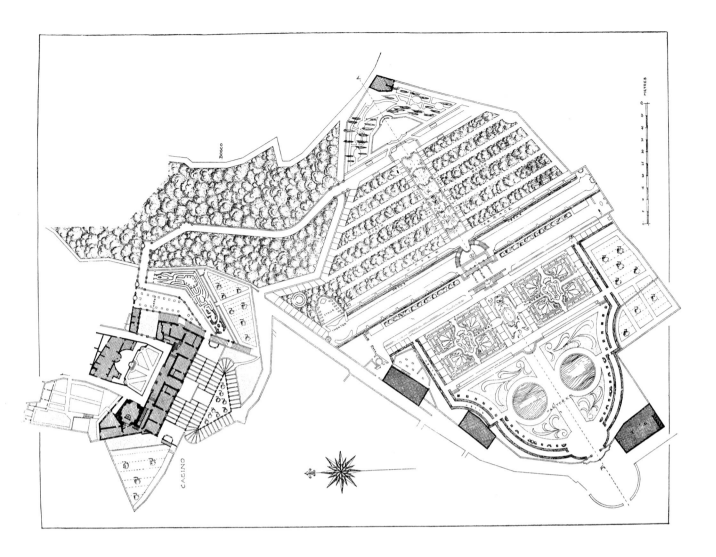

Compared with the seemingly level parterre, the triple flight of stairs with a double ramp at the end of this section appears positively monumental. Coloured mosaics reiterating the patterns of the flower beds and niches containing terracotta figures have been set into the façade of the supporting walls. Elaborate balustrades in a contrasting colour simultaneously protect and emphasize the steps and landings. The first terrace leads to an avenue of palms and the second to a path decorated by numerous sculptures. Pomona, the guardian goddess of the garden, stands guard at one end; at the other lies a small theatre roofed with leaves.

This visually so impressive staircase, one of the most dominant features of the garden and the point where the longitudinal and transverse axes intersect, leads not to the villa but to a water stairway which is a continuation of the central axis. It is crowned by Fama, the Roman personification of rumour, from whose horn water pours into a semicircular basin before flowing in cascades down the steps. Behind the statue there used to be secluded bathing pools whose ingenious waterworks sent guests into raptures. Nowadays this part of the garden has fallen into disrepair and it is only in the maze that watery jests still surprise the visitor.

The part of the garden which lies on the upper slopes features an extensive *bosco*, through which the water stairway channels a central aisle. Small footpaths laid out levelly at regular intervals, two larger avenues, cross the wood and lead to the house either through a little bamboo wood or past a maze. The visitor has an especially good view of one maze from the bridge which lies at the end of one of the avenues.

The steps, showing Mannerist ornamentation

Basin on the upper terrace

OPPOSITE PAGE:
Pergola-type bridge with "bull's eyes"

Bosco Sacro
BOMARZO
Bomarzo · Italy

Around the middle of the 16th century the architect Pirro Ligorio transformed a wood which lay near the family seat of the Prince of Orsini into a sculpture park, an art setting in the Renaissance sense. Bomarzo – this remarkable park – was a place of shady coolness in summer, so that it was a pleasure to spend time there; a place which not only displayed art but which was itself a work of art, created for the pleasure of its owner and to the envy of others.

Pier Francesco "Vicino" Orsini was, according to contemporary opinion, a commanding figure who preferred the excitement of battle to peaceful scholarship. But he was in no way uneducated. He read contemporary authors such as François Rabelais, Torquato Tasso and Ludovico Ariosto and was especially interested in books on the East Indies, treatises on longevity and romantic epics. That a man of his rank and period was also familiar with Greek and Roman mythology – the sculptures in his garden are ample proof – goes without saying. In addition to his literary preference, his letters in particular reveal him as a Mannerist.

In contrast to other Renaissance gardens, Bomarzo is not governed by the rules of order and geometry; it is equally futile to search for vantage points providing optically interesting vistas. The monumental stone sculptures are not arranged symmetrically, but rather stand where nature abandoned the erratic boulders from which Ligorio carved them. The large artificial lake and countless waterworks and fountains were famous, until eventually surpassed by those of the Villa d'Este. Today the fountains are dried up, and only the shoreline of the lake is still visible. Bomarzo is exclusively a rock garden.

Ignored for almost two hundred years, its surreal charm was only rediscovered in the mid-twentieth century by artists such as Salvador Dalí. A few years ago the present owner began extensive restoration work and has recently opened the garden to a wider public.

"You, who roam the world in search of sublime and fearful wonders, come hither and look upon terrible countenances, elephants, lions, bears, man-eaters and dragons." Thus the motto of the garden, carved in stone, which invites the visitor to tour the grounds. On another spot, the words cut into the pedestals of two sphinxes emphasize the desire of the owner to amaze the visitor: "Who does not pass this way wide-eyed will neither marvel at the seven famous wonders of the world."

A crooked house which stands at the former entrance to the park confuses the visitor's senses. It clearly upsets the rules of geometry and gravity and, when entered, the visitor's sense of orientation. The floors and walls seem to be frozen in the moment of collapse and the house to be sinking into the hillside. The sloping angle creates an undertow which sends everything – including one's internal equilibrium – reeling.

"You, who enter here, gather your thoughts and tell me whether such wonders are delusion or art." Whether art or illusion, the immense size of these stone sculptures is enough to impress the visitor.

Some have referred to literature in order to explain the significance of the sculptures. The colossus tearing a woman limb from limb could come from Ariosto's *Orlando Furioso*; the giants from Rabelais' *Gargantua and Pantagruel*; the stone dragons, the giant tortoises and the elephant from oriental fairy tales.

Another interpretation sees in these figures an allusion to the martial pasts of both Orsini and Rome, to their battles and victories. Mythological

Sculpture of the Roman goddess Ceres

explanations emphasize symbols of fertility and transience. The natural landscape of the park, with its visible cycles of growth and decay, lends special validity to this point of view. The sculptures of Ceres and Proserpina are particularly illustrative examples. Ceres, the Roman goddess of agriculture, corresponds in Greek mythology to Demeter, whose daughter Persephone – Proserpina to the Romans – was abducted by Hades while playing and taken to the underworld to be his bride. Demeter sought her daughter but without success. At last she withdrew from the world and allowed no more seeds to grow until Hermes, sent by Zeus, rescued Persephone from the underworld. Hades attempted, by means of a pomegranate, to bind her to his kingdom. The gods were obliged to intervene, and a compromise was agreed: Persephone would spend one third of the year in the underworld, the remaining two thirds on Mount Olympus. The rhythm of her migrations corresponds to the concept of seasonal change, of sowing and harvest.

Twenty years after the completion of the park, Vicino Orsini added a temple in memory of his deceased wife, Giulia Farnese, which gave the wood the epithet *Bosco Sacro* – sacred grove.

Elephant crushing a legionary

Dragon fighting its animal attackers

ABOVE:
Neptune

BELOW:
A petrified scream: the monster

OPPOSITE PAGE:
Pegasus, the winged horse

Of the magnificent châteaux of the Loire Valley, the last to be built – Villandry in 1536 – is comparatively rural, idyllic and intimate. It captivates with its simultaneous display of unassuming elegance and sturdy fortification – an ambivalence which is echoed in its intelligent architectural combinations of symmetrical and asymmetrical components.

Gardens of Château
VILLANDRY
Villandry · France

Since Villandry was largely spared the power struggles of the past, its special charm lies less in its historical significance than in the harmony of the grounds and in the originality of the garden. In his pamphlet "Villandry and its garden", the present owner has described the Renaissance-style garden as follows:

"A small valley with a stream running through it drops from a plateau towards the south. Its incline has made it possible to create three terraced garden levels: the uppermost level, where the water required to supply the moats, fountains and irrigations collects in a large mirror-shaped basin; the middle, ground level with the château reception rooms and an ornamental garden in which flowers are planted within a boxtree surround; and finally, beneath the windows of the west wing on the same level as the outhouses, probably the most original of the three gardens: the ornamental vegetable garden.

Each of the three gardens is surrounded and dominated by a roofed avenue (a vaulted cloister of trimmed lime trees and trellised vines). Thus the visitor is able to admire each detail while being protected from the rays of the Touraine sun, which can be extremely strong in high summer. Here we see the application of the principle formulated by Olivier de Serres: the gardens are best viewed from above looking down, either from neighbouring buildings or from raised terraces surrounding the beds.

The three gardens appear to be contained:
bordered to the east by the château and the high terraces which stand out against the slope of the hill, and whose verdant foliage rises almost 50 metres above the garden;

Pattern and detailed view of the four beds of the Garden of Love

bordered to the west by the village and its old church, overlooking the vegetable garden from the opposite side of the valley and facing the château. Neither the village nor the church are thus far from the manor house, in keeping with – subsequently abandoned – mediaeval tradition; bordered to the north by the outhouses: chicken yard and stables, whose high walls protect the vegetable garden from the coldest winds; and finally to the south by the countryside: here, a natural transition is created by a large orchard which rides gently towards the fields on the plateau.

Thus everything at Villandry has been so designed as to give the château residents a clear, compact view of the necessities of material and spiritual life in a vista which is a joy to behold."

Villandry's Italian character is emphasized not only by its design clarity

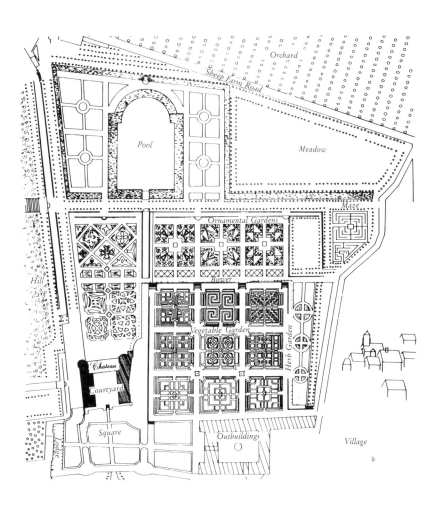

Sketch of the grounds

and the close relationship between château and garden, but in particular by its fountains, its architecture, its flower-bedecked arches and the way in which the herb and flower garden are enclosed by dwarf boxtrees. Villandry was famous for its vegetable garden before the 16th century was out. The Cardinal of Aragon, who visited the garden in 1570, wrote to the Pope "that he had seen lettuces that were even finer than (those) in Rome".

The engravings of the French architect Jacques Andronet Du Cerceau give us an idea of how the decorative patterns of the ornamental flower and vegetable beds in Villandry, and in many other château gardens (for example Blois, Amboise and Chenonceaux in the Loire valley, Anet, Gaillon and Fontainebleau near Paris) must have looked during the 16th century. He proves that useful gardens could be designed according to the same formal and aesthetic principles as ornamental gardens. Joachim Carvallo, the grandfather of the château's present owner, used these engravings as the basis for his reconstruction – at the beginning of the century – of Villandry's vegetable garden. The artistic arrangement of a noble Renaissance vegetable garden can today be seen only at Villandry.

ABOVE:
View of the ornamental gardens and château

BELOW:
Detailed view of the vegetable garden

OPPOSITE PAGE:
Ornamental garden with village church behind

II. The construction of individuality

The thankless task of completing the Belvedere courtyard and, after Michelangelo's death, taking over the building of St. Peter's fell to Pirro Ligorio. In the case of the basilica he decided against the Greek cross which Michelangelo, respecting Bramante's original idea, had favoured as the best and only appropriate solution. Despite this, by taking over their unfinished projects, Ligorio came so close to two of the most important architects of his age that his own work was thereby decisively influenced.

Around 1550 Ligorio started planing one of his major works, the Villa d'Este in Tivoli. It can be seen here, as in so many other examples, that the design of a garden in the modern age followed in only a very limited fashion from existing natural conditions. Cardinal Ippolito d'Este, who had commissioned the project, was totally unconcerned by the natural topography of the location. For him the unambiguous point of reference was the villa which he had built on the summit of the town's hill. He demanded that the garden be laid out in strict symmetry to the main axis of the building. This meant the extensive underpinning and artifical filling of almost half the entire garden. Thus it is easy to see that the concept of the garden does not arise, in the first instance, from any conception of "nature" or "naturalness" – and has nothing at all to do with "divine creation". The unity of villa, garden and park is shown to be much more the self-presentation of man as a free individuality.

It may seem unusual to think of a garden as illustrating a uniform, anthropomorphic idea. Today, especially, the tendency is to appreciate only such elements as terraces, flights of stairs, fountains and exedras in the various gardens and, if necessary, to praise the harmonious aesthetics of their composition. A category such as "individuality" might be expected in sculpture and painting, which concern the portrayal of man. It would be less familiar in the context of pure architecture, churches, villas and residences, while under garden architecture one normally understands a purely applied art of secondary status. In Ligorio's day, however, people thought differently. His contemporaries held garden design to be an autonomous art, no less important than painting and even more important than sculpture. It is worth putting aside for a while the prejudices of later generations and to consider the reasons for this high esteem.

While thinking of garden architecture as the presentation of an artistic world, we should not misunderstand this as false idealism. Art does not lay down the law to nature, but neither does it accept nature's laws as absolute. In the architectural design of gardens, art and nature meet in interaction. This confrontation is characterized by a decided element of aggression. In the case of the Italian and French gardens, the argument was clearly decided in favour of art and the mind. In the case of the English landscape gardens, however, the emphasis seems to shift – a point we will return to later. For now it should be noted that, since the early 16th century, "nature" has only been employed in garden architecture as an idea which is caught up in an interdependent process with the ideas of art and the mind. The filling of whole areas, the diversion of rivers, the artificial irrigation of large regions, the clearing and planting of complete woods are part of this process. These endeavours do not offend the idea of nature, but simply allow it to flourish only in those areas where art concedes that it will do so to the greatest effect.

Garden of the *Villa d'Este*, Tivoli, Italy

The ideational scale of these frequently immense undertakings – a factor which must also be stressed – lies not in the aesthetic intentions of the artist, and still less in the specifications of the customer. When we talk here of "individuality", we do not mean the self-realization of individual persons. Any accusation of anthropomorphism is therefore inappropriate. Rather, when we talk of the garden's individuality, we mean that the garden has its own internal stringency and homogeneous legitimacy. Bramante laid the framework for this. With the Villa d'Este Ligorio took up Bramante's ideas and developed them further.

The concept of the *boundary* is a useful touchstone in the attempt to order the various elements and aspects of the overall plan. This concept had already made an appearance in Bramante's work, in the way he completely enclosed the Belvedere courtyard within tall architectural elements. Ligorio likewise placed a clear boundary right around the Villa d'Este so that it appeared from the outside to be one single physical entity.

But the boundary is also important for what lies within and asserts itself as an ordering, separating and unifying principle. For the general structure of the Villa d'Este Ligorio returned to Bramante's tripartite form: the lower area is here a garden laid out on the level; diametrically opposite and higher up is the villa with a terrace lying before it; between the two is a slope divided into five smaller sections. The lower level, is dedicated like the tournament ground in the *cortile* to the idea of corpo-reality and physis. One could say that this is where nature is most itself. The square centrepiece of this lower level is the *Giardino delle Semplici* enclosed by a paling. This sounds like an elementary lesson from a textbook of logic, which begins with the simple and gradually moves on to the more complex. Strange as it sounds, this is exactly what happens. The large square is divided by two artfully vaulted pathways into four equally sized compartments. Each of these is itself again divided and contains rows of carefully-demarcated herb beds. Access to these beds is strictly regulated by means of fences and pergolas. All licence is excluded. The whole area could have been designed by Petrus Ramus, the famous logician of the day, who sought to reestablish the unity of mathematics and nature which had been lost in the late Middle Ages.

The pergolas, however, also serve a quite different function. Since the grounds are laid out symmetrically to a central axis, everyone who entered through the central portal would have a clear view up to the villa. Precisely such a view is prevented by the arched lathing of the pergolas. The complete grounds cannot be viewed as a whole from below and are thus not accessible to all comers. Although the body develops, in its naturalness, its fundamental components, it must nevertheless submit to a strict order, the rule of the mind, if it is to become active and effective. It cannot claim mastery over the whole.

The danger of potential hubris on the part of the body, of insistence upon independence, is shown by the four neighbouring squares to the sides. These are *mazes*, and their function is by no means purely decorative. By the time the visitor has reached them, he has already virtually lost sight of the central axis and thus any possible orientation to the upper level. Since the healing powers of the herbs have now also been left behind, the body has to fend for itself and the inevitable happens: it becomes lost in the hopeless of its self-conceit and inadequacy. The danger is clearly described. These mazes may nevertheless not be compared to Dantesque

circles of hell. Man's own actions and decisions take him inside, and not a decree from above. Furthermore, each maze has an exit. The strict geometry of the aberration experienced indicates that only reason can point the way out of an entanglement with foolishness, and that the struggle against unreason is itself a worthwhile spiritual occupation.

Garden of the *Villa d'Este*, Tivoli, Italy

On the other side of the mazes Ligorio placed an area of undifferentiated deciduous trees. They represent the periphery of individuality and indicate the possibility that the individual may very quickly become lost in the indistinguishability of the multitude if he strays any further from the central axis and loses sight of the path to the upper level entirely.

The "boundary" plays an important role in this lower level, too: a fence encloses the central square, the mazes are nothing other than intertwined border lines and the areas of deciduous trees are clearly delineated. Quite apart from the architectural changes which have since been made, the present-day state of the trees of the Villa d'Este sadly no longer permits any sense of the boundaries between the individual areas. The trees have grown too high and thus hinder the awareness of leaving or approaching the important axes and boundaries of the garden. One of these boundaries lies between the lower garden and the beginning of the incline. At this important transition point, there is not simply a staircase leading upwards to the next part of the grounds. Instead, Ligorio employed four rectangular ponds to create a clearly visible lateral axis. He thus introduces the element of water which had played such an important role for Bramante. Tivoli is famous for its waterworks. What it is vital to consider here, however, is the idea which prompted Ligorio to employ water solely at the middle level of the garden.

It was Bramante who helped water in its transition from the mediaeval atrium to its integration – in the style of classical antiquity – into ascending terraces. In the case of Ligorio, however, there is no longer any reference to either classical or mediaeval models. Tivoli champions water in all its most modern symbolism. Bramante had already recognized that the polarity of mind and nature was the inner characteristic of individuality. Within this tension, the mind acquires the power of *generality*, and nature in all its manifestations the strength of *unity*. As has already been shown, it is not a question of the dualistic struggle between two equal principles. There is absolutely no direct connection between the two, thanks to the presence of a third, self-contained and independent sphere which both divides and mediates between them. This is the sphere of *particularity*, which has both a general and a specific side, without however losing its independence. Bramante had indicated this intermediate stage with a single, very simple terrace. Ligorio went much further. He extended it to a whole world, which developed in all directions and dimensions with unlimited generosity and freedom. Ligorio had the profound insight to realize that real life takes place neither solely in the world of the body nor in the world of the mind. Neither the rigid squares of the lower level nor the somewhat aloof villa demand such one-sidednesses. It is only in the intermediate stage, and in the particularization which it brings, that the true tensions and charms, efforts and rewards of life in the modern age lie.

Ligorio found in *water* the formal architectural element which best corresponded with this view. It is light and heavy at the same time, and thus half-way between mind and matter. As a fluid, it corresponds to the "pneumatic" quality of the spiritual; it is all-penetrating, supple, light and transparent, a source of life, subject to no barriers. These properties are particularly suitable for creating visual analogies of the wasteful, outpouring as well as reviving powers of the spirit. Plunging waters and large, cool, transparent pools thus form one side of Ligorio's fountain architecture.

On the other hand, of course, water is no pneuma, and Ligorio was well aware of this. It is inert, sluggish matter and as such a separate element of nature. Ligorio depicted this pure being and self-composure of nature in the form of calm pools, which dissolve the solidness of matter into fluidity without thereby relinquishing their materiality. They are thus rightly placed on the border between the lower and middle areas.

Ligorio used the boundary function of the pools in yet another way. Their alignment creates a bolt, shot across the linear course of the central axis like a lateral axis. It is thus made very clear that a new, consciously different level begins here. At the same time, Ligorio yet again draws attention away from the central axis by placing large waterworks at the two extremes of the lateral axis: an imposing water organ and a (no longer existing) waterwork, sited on a man-made promontory. When one beholds the contrast between the peaceful pools and the water works at their ends – a contrast reinforced by two heavily symbolic meta-sudan pillars in the two central pools – it becomes clear that water as a boundary both divides and surpasses itself. The art and artistry of man can overcome the natural weight of water and transport it upwards, in other words towards the mind – hence the water organ with its music – and then allowing it to follow its own natural inclinations and fall back to earth. This seems to me the real idea behind Ligorio's fountains. They portray the manifold, infinitely imaginative processes of particularization between "mind" and "nature": the wearisome path toward the summit, as suggested by the Sweating Columns, the force of the free-falling waters and the higher orders which are reflected in the water's purity. At the same time, however, they give an idea of the tremendous forces which men of the modern age can mobilize and channel. Ligorio even claimed that man had to set these powers in motion in order to assert the freedom of his individuality.

I do not intend to examine in detail each of Ligorio's inventions. Their praises have been sung throughout the ages, and the richness of their inventiveness continues to amaze and astound visitors today. Only two aspects should be singled out for attention, since they are of particular significance for the development of the idea of the garden. The whole middle area, with its pool and fountains and its fruit trees growing on the slopes, serves the improvement and refinement of nature. One should nevertheless resist the temptation of seeing it as a *locus amoenus*, an idyllic Arcadia. The world of particularization and definition, as found in the Villa d'Este, is a dangerous land of adventure whose heart houses a dragon and which breaks down into notable historical and political extremes.

These extremes are indicated in the magnificent Avenue of the Hundred Fountains. The avenue forms the second lateral axis; one reaches it immediately after passing the dragon. The relief decorations set among the many small fountains are derived from Ovid's *Metamorphoses* and symbolize the continually self-renewing process of metamorphosis between man and nature. The *Metamorphoses* portray a world which is anything but idyllic. They are characterized by cruelty, inevitability and death and hence appear again and again in art in forms laden with historical significance. The Avenue of the Hundred Fountains is bordered on one side by a miniature allegory: the Tiber, the she-wolf, Roma enthroned; opposite is the *Fontana dell'Ovato*, perhaps the most beautiful of the garden's fountains, also known as *la Regina delle Fontane*. On the fountain are depicted the winged horse Pegasus, the Sibylla Albunea and some nymphs. This layout transforms the avenue into a temporal axis, providing a co-ordinate to the spatial longitudinal axis. Ippolito loved to trace the house and lineage of the Este family from Roman origins. The allegory of Rome represents the past, from which time – in the form of countless little fountains and metamorphoses – has rolled on to reach the most splendid of the fountains, which with its visionary and winged Pegasus powerfully bubbles the future of the House of d'Este. The coat of arms on the floor of the fountain makes the interpretation unambiguous.

The dimension of time, with all its political implications, was not merely one of the Cardinal's little quirks. It was to become a major dimension of all large gardens. Without its ideas of time and of history, Versailles would be unthinkable. The emergence of the English landscape garden likewise cannot be explained without reference to their historicity and the spirit of the political opposition. Here in Tivoli, the self-containedness of individuality prohibits the idea of history from disturbing the internal equilibrium of the gardens as a whole. By keeping time away from the spatial longitudinal axis, indeed by having time cut right across space, an ideational standstill is reached. The past becomes an allegory, history a magnificent avenue and the future a fountain which feeds from its own waters.

The second aspect which deserves consideration is the dragon which gives the garden's central fountain its name and whose magnificent waters can be seen from afar. In order to understand that it was not merely a decorative element, but rather had a very real connection with figures of contemporary art, we should remember that Ippolito d'Este was not just Pirro Ligorio's patron but was also the "Successor to Hercules" to whom Ariosto dedicated his *Orlando furioso*. This great epic was published in

1532. It is rightly considered one of the most important and influential literary works of the 16th century. Ariosto's masterpiece was based on a work by Boiardo, *Orlando innamorato*, a product of the previous century which, with its plot consisting of many brilliantly interwoven strands, still belonged to the genre of late courtly epic. Ariosto did not merely continue where Boiardo had left off. Although he took over most of Boiardo's characters, he broke fundamentally away from tradition and made Orlando a prototype of the modern hero, as Cervantes did a short time later with Don Quixote. The essential trait of his hero is not love, but rather madness, the futility of his endeavours, his lack of realism, his ranting and raging. Then there is the other side, a mirror held up to Dante. The beloved woman is no Beatrice. She is called Angelica and is the very opposite of pure and virginal. She is loved by many men, and is willing to accept any of their offers if she sees personal advantage in doing so. The "love" which she arouses in her admirers is no Dantesque piety but rather a wild passion, which robs them of their reason and sometimes even their lives.

Viewed in the light of *Orlando furioso*, many of the creations of Italian

Bomarzo, Italy
Echidna sculpture

garden design no longer seem strange. Familiar scenery and fully-intelligible situations appear: dragons rise up out of the water, swords and helmets gleam from enchanted springs, women lose their way in forests and mazes, healing herbs are laid on fatal wounds. Fantasy knew no bounds. Nor was it merely unreal; it must have corresponded to an actual awareness of life and the time. Bomarzo is one of the most original creations to arise out of the Ariostan spirit. It is suspected that Ligorio also designed this park. It would certainly be logical: as an apotheosis of particularity. Today, Bomarzo appears to many as a gallery of curios. For the contemporaries of Ariosto and Tasso, however, it would have been much less strange to suddenly encounter a giantess, an enormous tortoise, a dragon or some other monster in the middle of a *sacro bosco*, and to find a bewitched house at an odd angle and other such wonders. In those days, people probably expected to hear the cries for help of an abducted woman coming from the house and would have found it quite normal for a Rinaldo or a Ruggiero to rush into the house to do battle with the oriental magician. In Ligorio's time, almost everyone who ventured a walk through one of the great Italian gardens must have been familiar with the pleasance of Alcina and the magical garden of Armida, and will have taken into account the perils of his venture:

> Now though effects prove not in all alike,
> Yet all are mad in sort, all go astray,
> As in a wilderness, where men do seek,
> And more and more in seeking loose their way;
> Wherefore let no man this my wish mislike
> In whom fond love shall carie long the sway
> I wish for due reward such doting dolts,
> like wilfull pris'ners, store of iron bolts.
> (*Orlando furioso*, 24th Book, translated by Sir John Harrington, 1633)

The construction of individuality in the modern age has left all connection with Church and religion far behind. It has led instead to a world of arts but this world is neither very idyllic nor very aesthetic, cheerful or charming. On the contrary, it is full of necessities and mathematical rigour. Danger lurks everywhere and there is no guarantee of survival. The unity of body and mind is the ultimate idea of the Italian garden. It is a completely newly constituted sphere: particularity. But it can itself furnish only individuality, in whose interior lurks madness and which faces the outside world alone and unaided: master of itself and slave to this same selfhood.

FOLLOWING PAGE:
View of the garden front of Schloss Brühl
Brühl, Germany

Baroque and Rococo Gardens

Gardens of Château
VAUX-LE-VICOMTE
Melun · France

The plans for the gardens of Vaux-le-Vicomte marked the beginning of André Le Nôtre's meteoric career. In 1661 Nicolas Fouquet summoned the almost fifty-year-old member of a great gardening dynasty to Vaux. Up until then, Le Nôtre's main occupations had been the care of the Tuileries Gardens and the study of perspective. This quiet horticulturalist was now transformed into an artist, who, from nothing – three villages had to be bought up and then demolished to make space for the gardens – created gardens which aroused not only admiration but envy.

Le Nôtre's patron, Nicolas Fouquet, a typically status-hungry man of the *grand siècle*, was finance minister under Mazarin and at the peak of his career. In the middle of the 17th century, he appointed the architect and friend of Le Nôtre, Louis Le Valu, and the painter Charles Le Brun to create his château, a project they completed – employing vast quantities of both staff and money – within just five years.

It was a beautiful estate whose magnificence was memorably underlined by a spectacular celebration. The young King Louis XIV was invited to a second celebration; it confirmed the rumours he had heard about the wealth of Vaux-le-Vicomte and strengthened his suspicions that the finance minister could hardly have paid for such regal luxury. One month later, Fouquet was arrested and sentenced to life imprisonment. Louis XIV had much of the removable furnishings – vases, statues etc. – brought to Versailles, for which he had already engangled Le Nôtre, Le Vau and Le Brun. The château of Vaux-le-Vicomte, abandoned, fell into disrepair. It was only at the end of the 19th century that its new owner, the industrialist Alfred Sommier, undertook its comprehensive restoration.

Perspective view of the waterfalls
Engraving by Israel Sylvestre

Radial park avenues lead to a spacious exedra-shaped approach in front of an entrance courtyard partitioned by grilles and decorative balustrades. Stables on both sides conceal working quarters and kitchen gardens. The palace itself stands on a man-made terrace and – like other French châteaux of the time – is surrounded by a wide moat. To its sides are simple parterre gardens decorated with fountains. A drawbridge leads from the terrace on which the château stands over the moat to the main garden, which

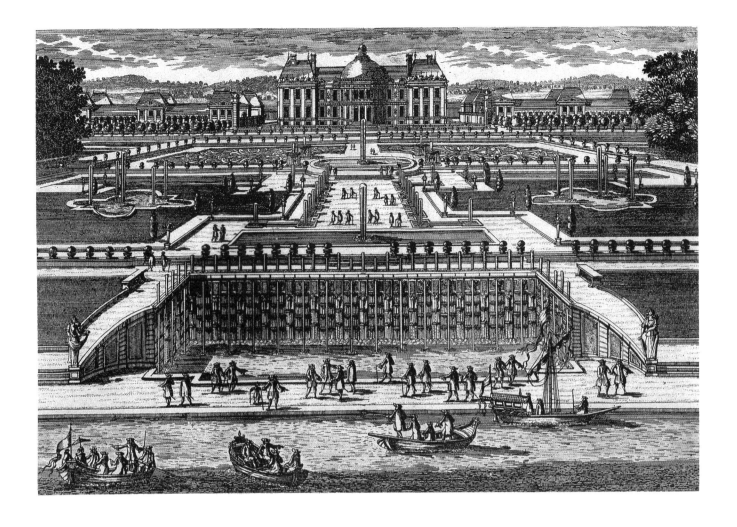

Large waterfall, garden and château
Engraving by Aveline

runs gently down to an impressive example of mock architecture before rising steeply again.

One of Vaux-le-Vicomte's most remarkable features is the presentation of perspective, produced by a skilful use of the existing landscape combined with calculated sensory illusion. Woods on either side of the grounds form a contrast to the flat, ordered layout of the gardens. The central avenue was planned as the main symmetrical axis. Near the main building, it passes between two double *parterres de broderies* featuring (now changed) ornamental patterns of box. These are flanked by slightly higher, simpler parterres. A fountain at the far end of the middle pathway and two canals to the sides conclude the first level of the garden.

On the east side the lateral axis leads to a three-level water grille, formerly used as a stage setting. The edges of the pathway were originally accentuated by small channels featuring countless playing fountains. Today, these have been replaced by grass borders. The path runs along past two lawn parterres with broad-based fountains before reaching a large, square basin, whose position was accurately calculated for its optical effect. Standing behind it, one sees the façade of the château mirrored in its waters. Standing in front of it, one has the impression that the grottoes which are part of the architecture of the terrace are resting on the edge of the basin and pouring water into it. The entire width of the main garden is bounded by the River Anqueil, here transformed into a transverse canal.

On the château side, although not visible from it, the canal is lined by waterfalls, while on the opposite side, behind the canal extension, ramps and flights of steps surround the grotto.

FOLLOWING DOUBLE PAGE:
View of the château and grounds

101

ABOVE:
Stairway leading to the terrace above the grotto;
detailed view of the Anqueil Allegory

ABOVE RIGHT:
Sculptural group in one of the side basins

RIGHT:
Grotto with allegory of the River Anqueil

FOLLOWING DOUBLE PAGE:
View of parterres with ornamental box hedges

Gardens of
VERSAILLES
Versailles · France

"Your Majesty knows that, in the absence of acts of war, nothing shows the greatness and spirit of a ruler to better advantage than architecture," Jean-Baptiste Colbert wrote in the autumn of 1665 to his king, Louis XIV. The splendid celebrations at Vaux-le-Vicomte in summer 1661 had been a challenge and a provocation for the young king. All that was needed was a suitable framework for even more splendid festivities, one which would put all those of the past completely in the shade.

In the Baroque period, court festivals were a definite metaphor of life. They were designed and performed by the greatest and best artists of the age. They became total works of art which rendered homage to the sovereignty of the ruler. One feast day followed another; there was no shortage of suitable excuses and no limit to the extravagance. The Baroque was an epoch of fast living; the reverse side of its ever more gigantic and grandiose parties – and the psychological reason for them – was the flight from an inner emptiness. Today, a walk through the gardens of Versailles shows how artistically empty spaces could be filled, even although much of it is mere sham. One of the most famous of the celebrations at Versailles was the *Divertissement de Versailles* which took place in summer 1674 on the occasion of the conquest of Burgundy. Richard Alewyn described its magnificence in his book, *Das grosse Welttheater*:

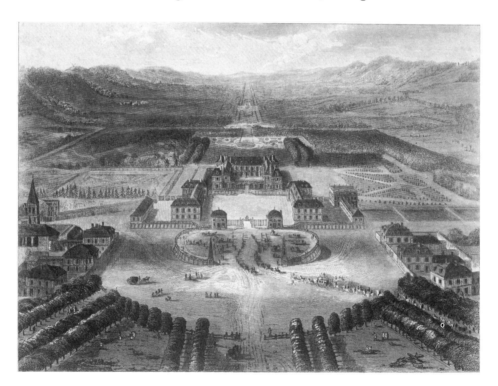

The palace grounds in 1664

"On the evening of the first day, after a snack in the Bosquet du Marais, everyone enjoyed a performance of *Alceste* for which Quinault had written the text and Lully the music. The performance took place under the night sky in the Cour de Marbre which was festively illuminated and decorated with flowers and little orange trees. Afterwards there was a *souper de medianoche* in the palace followed by a ball which lasted until dawn.

"On the next day a *salon de verdure* was erected in the garden in front of the Trianon, an octagonal arbour with an open roof and a view of the avenue. The *Eglogue de Versailles*, an interlude also written by Quinault and Lully was performed. Then a *souper* on a floating island in the middle of the great canal. The island was behind bars. The meal was eaten by the

Grand Trianon
Engraving by Aveline, 1687/88

light of torches which reflected the sparkle of the silver a thousand times over and to the accompaniment of the sound of the water rising and falling. On the third evening there was a snack in the menagerie followed by a boat trip on the canal with lights and music. Afterwards Molière's *Malade Imaginaire* was performed in the grotesque setting of a grotto.

"The snack on the fourth evening was eaten in the water theatre. 160 fruit-trees, 120 baskets with bread, pastries and jam, 400 bowls of ice-cream and 1000 caraffes containing liqueurs were set up on the three steps which surrounded it. In the background burbled the waterworks. A theatre was erected in another part of the park. They played, they sang and they danced: *The Feasts of Amor and Bacchus*. A night drive through the park with torches and fireworks on the great canal followed and finally a *medianoche* in the marble courtyard. The table was wonderfully decorated with food, flowers and stones.

"On the fifth day a performance of Racine's *Iphigénie* in the orangery was followed by magical illuminations on the great canal, created by the court artist, Le Brun. An obelisk of light borne by golden gryphons rose from the water, a sun shining from its tip. At its foot was a dragon majestically beating its wings. One saw humiliated prisoners and the triumphant king. All of a sudden 1,500 cannon were fired. The banks of the canal and the steps of the waterfall were brightly lit up, the dragon breathed torrents of fire, red and blue smoke pouring from its nostrils, its mouth and its eyes, lightening flashed over the water, and finally 5,000 rockets were set off simultaneously, briefly forming a vault of light over the canal before sinking to the earth in a shower of stars.

"Around one o'clock in the morning on the final night – one of the darkest and quietest of the summer – the whole park was flooded with light: the terraces, the open ground, the pools and the canal were lined with shimmering strings of pearls, the fountains gleamed mysteriously, the canal looked like an enormous crystal mirror with the façade of an enchanted palace glowing at the end of it. The entire court clambered into gondolas. Neptune, drawn by four sea-horses, came forward to greet his guests. As the music reached the palace, figures standing on it began to sing sweetly and to dance in the heavy scent of the July night beneath the sultry sky. Thus ended the last of the great celebrations at Versailles."

Versailles' history began in the same year as Nicolas Fouquet's fall from grace. Then small and unprepossessing, it reminded Louis XIV of the happy days of his youth. He had often found refuge in the small hunting lodge built by his father, Louis XIII, and now decided to preserve it – not least for his rendezvous with Mademoiselle de la Valière. But however strong the King's love of Versailles, its location and climatic conditions were a powerful argument against making it the setting for a garden so prestigious that it would put all the gardens that had ever existed in the western world in the shade.

Neither cost nor effort was spared in the transformation of the marshland at Versailles into a splendid work of art, worthy of a Sun King. André Le Nôtre began work on the garden in 1662; its basic design already included all its most important elements, from the northerly main parterre garden to the great east-west axis. The original castle, a building with three wings made of brick and ashlar and surrounded by a moat, was extended several times during the 1660s and 1670s until its dimensions finally reflected the self-image of the most powerful king in Europe.

A system of lateral and longitudinal axes, like the other basic elements ordered and symmetrical in their orientation, forms the framework of the grounds.

The main axis, on which lie the garden's main points of iconological emphasis, emerges in front of the palace in the shape of the *Parterre d'Eau*. It was only after various preliminary stages that it acquired its present form: two parallel basins in which the buildings are reflected. They are decorated with groups of cherubs, nymphs and allegorical depictions of the major rivers of France. An avenue leads via stairs and two ramps decorated with statues to the *Bassin Latone*, a circular fountain of four marble steps. From here a narrow, gently falling carpet of green grass, the *Tapis-Vert*, lined by various baskets, leads in a straight line to the *Bassin d'Apollon*, begun in 1663. Apollo, the god of light, moral order and all things lofty and noble, is the central figure in the imagery of Versailles and a symbol of the king himself. The huge basin, completed by Jean-Baptiste Tuty following Le Brun's plans, is 75 metres long and 110 metres wide. Apollo, in a sun carriage drawn by four fiery steeds and accompanied by Tritons and dolphins, charges fearlessly, almost aggressively towards the palace.

The *Grand Canal*, in the shape of a cross, begun in 1667/68 and completed in 1680, brings the main axis to an end. It is 1,670 metres long and at its widest point – where it opens out into an octagonal basin – it measures 92 metres. The lateral is 1,070 metres long and 75 metres wide. On festive occasions and night-time banquets an entire fleet of gondolas waited to take guests on pleasure cruises.

View of the palace from the garden

OPPOSITE PAGE:
Detailed view of the colonnades
by Aardouin Mansart

FOLLOWING DOUBLE PAGE:
Four views of the Fountain of
Apollo

OPPOSITE PAGE:
Detailed view of the Dragon
Fountain

RIGHT:
Detailed view of the Fountain of
Saturn

BELOW:
Detailed view of the Fountain of
Latona

Gardens of the
BELVEDERE
Vienna · Austria

In 1693, following his successful defeat of the Turks, Prince Eugène of Savoy acquired the northerly slopes of a vineyard which lay at the gates of liberated Vienna with the intention of building himself a summer residence there. The thirty-year-old prince was regarded as the greatest general of his age. As well as being at the very centre of the political arena he was a knowledgeable and influential collector and patron of the arts who actively participated in the intellectual life of the period.

In his youth, Prince Eugène had lived at Versailles with his mother, who for some years had been a member of the inner circle at the court of Louis XIV. Both French influence and the desire to compete with his personal enemy, Louis XIV, are clearly reflected in the building Prince Eugène sponsored, although the result was in no sense merely a formal or iconographic derivative. Prince Eugène commissioned the architect Johann Lucas von Hildebrandt, the antipode of the great Baroque architect Johann Bernhard Fischer von Erlach, to design his country residence. At first, work proceeded slowly. The first part of the garden was completed in 1706 and ten years later, after a construction period of two years, the palace was finally finished. In 1717, while the plans for a second, far more prestigious building further up the hill were being drawn up, the prince engaged Dominique Girard, a pupil of André Le Nôtre's, to give the final artistic touch to the reconstruction work thereby necessitated. Apart from a few lost decorative figures and fountain groups, the garden can be viewed essentially unchanged today.

The main garden is narrow; only as wide as the two palaces which enclose it at its top and bottom ends. On its long sides, the garden is lined by hedges and raised walkways. Viewed from the Upper Belvedere, the garden appears laid out in accordance with all the rules of garden design. Viewed from the Lower Belvedere, constantly changing perspectives make it a visual experience, with the House of Savoy as focal point.

The central axis runs without a break from the *sala terrena* of the Upper Belvedere to the central hall of the Lower. The central axis is crucial in this garden; it unites all the vital structural elements, even those that seem far, and thus symbolizes the Baroque desire to synthesize the horticultural, architectural and artistic elements. The intensification of ornamental elements both emphasizes the splendour of the Upper Belvedere and suggests the garden was to be viewed from the Lower.

The main garden is divided by waterfalls and ramps into three interconnected sections. The lowest level begins with four thickets of fast-growing hornbeam hedges which help to create an intimate atmosphere. These surround lawn parterres, of which the two outer were decorated by fountains depicting scenes from mythology. This level is regarded as symbolizing the elemental, which rises up to the divine sphere of the Upper Belvedere. The lower waterfall with its grotto-like architecture and its many minor sea-gods picks up this theme. The waterfall is built into the retaining wall of the first terrace and, viewed from below, looks like a pedestal on top of which the Upper Belvedere sits like a castle in the air. The second area of the garden is reached via broad ramp stairways at each side. Here, between sloping embankments, lies a somewhat sunken garden featuring two oval pools and various groups of statues depicting scenes from the life of Hercules and Apollo. The large cascade which connects this area with the upper level pours down over five steps and is decorated with the figures of major sea-gods. Two sunken *parterres de*

Bird's-eye view of the grounds
Copperplate engraving by Salomon Kleiner,
1731–1740

broderies containing sculptures and fountains are the most splendid part of the garden and thus closest to the palace.

The orangery in the Small Belvedere garden, which tapers off to a point in the spandrel between the lower part of the main garden, the Lower Belvedere and the garden of Count Fondi-Mansfeld, was introduced at an early stage. In winter, a mobile window wall and a roof on rollers were used to transform this orangery into a pavilion, which could be heated with large ovens. Other exotic plants, of which the prince was an enthusiastic collector, were kept in the Great Conservatory. Next to the orangery is an ornamental area on a slightly higher level, bordered on the slope side by small pavilions and treillages covered with ivy, vine and climbing rose. Its point ends in hedge boskets with an aviary and *boulingrin*.

From the south side of the Upper Belvedere a trapeziform courtyard opens out into a reservoir, a carefully designed kitchen garden and a menagerie for exotic animals, their cages aligned in a fan shape.

FOLLOWING DOUBLE PAGE:
Great Cascade and Upper Belvedere

119

TOP RIGHT:
Sculpture bordering the Great Cascade

RIGHT:
Palace and gardens with the city of Vienna in
the background

PAGE 124:
Details of Pan and the Sphinxes

PAGE 125:
Upper Belvedere in the evening light

Gardens of
HET LOO
Apeldoorn · The Netherlands

The history of Het Loo and its magnificent garden in the French style begins in the second half of the 17th century with the hunting rights which were granted to William of Orange for Veluwe, a lonely spot which was rich in game. In order to increase his sporting pleasure, William purchased Het Loo, and the extensive conversion and rebuilding of his new hunting residence was begun in 1684. The Dutch architect Jacob Roman supervised the building work, which was probably first based on plans by the Academie d'Architecture in Paris, and subsequently on designs by the Huguenot Daniel Marot. The garden was as carefully planned and constructed as the palace.

Seven years later, after his coronation as King William III of England, he extended the garden, adding a second part, the upper garden. His successors again altered the grounds, adding a hothouse for exotic plants, a tea pavilion and a bathhouse. It was not long before all the innovative possibilities of garden architecture were exhausted. Lack of upkeep due to the expense involved, and structural measures taken by different owners who had lost sight of the architectural integrity of the grounds as a whole, led over the course of time to their gradual decline and decay.

In 1970 it was decided to turn Het Loo into a national monument: the modifications of the 19th and 20th centuries were to be reversed and the palace and garden reconstructed true to the original on the basis of old engravings and accounts. In summer 1984, work was completed and the grounds opened to the public.

The designs for both the house and the gardens are indebted to the aesthetic ideals of the 17th century. Virtually everything is symmetrical and laid out in parallel. The central axis originally ran not only from the forecourt via the palace and through the garden, but also passed beyond the colonnade at the end of the upper garden and finally, by way of a kilometre-long avenue of elm trees, led up to a wooden obelisk. The central axis divides the grounds into a west and an east half which are virtual mirror images of each other, in some cases down to the smallest detail.

Leaving the palace on the ground floor, one passes through a gilded wrought-iron gate which stands in the exact centre of the lower section, and then descends an exedra-shaped flight of outdoor steps to reach the garden. Eight rectangular parterres, of which the filigree ornamentation of the inner four is particularly striking, are here arranged in rows of two. On the far side of the lateral axis, which runs parallel to the gate, lies the Queen's Garden to the east. A network of *berceaut* (pergolas), only half of which it was possible to reconstruct, combined with the presence of exclusively "feminine" flowers such as columbine and lilies – symbols of the Virgin Mary – give this part of the garden its private character.

The King's Garden, dedicated to the former master of the household, begins, like its pendant, with a double *parterre de broderies* and fruit trees trained over espaliers. The colours of the flowers, red and blue, symbolize the House of Orange-Nassau and pick up the colours used in the master bedroom in the adjoining west wing. A *boulingrin* – a broad grassy area used for ball games – replaces the pergolas in the Queen's Garden.

A number of fountains and waterworks with mythological and allegorical figures accentuate the central and intersecting points of this area. The most important and most beautiful fountains – the main fountain is dedicated to Venus and Cupid – are reserved for the broad central avenue and give the generally rather flat grounds of Het Loo an additional, vertical dimension. The avenue is lined by narrow canals, which carry water to various destinations within the garden.

In the upper part of the garden, the main avenue passes small rectangular parterres before reaching one of the showpieces of the grounds, the King's Fountain. A jet of water, 13 metres high and surrounded by several smaller fountains, plunges into an octagonal pool with a diameter of 32 metres.

Clay pipes with decorative emblems bring the water for the fountains in the upper garden from higher regions some kilometres away. The fountains in the lower garden are fed from a pond in the park, so that at Het Loo, in contrast to other gardens such as Versailles, the water in the fountains is always fresh. Both upper and lower gardens are surrounded by embankments and colonnades, which replace the typical Dutch canals found in watery regions of the Netherlands. The walls probably also serve the practical purpose of keeping out the sand which is constantly swept across the landscape. Outside the enclosure, the park provides further diversions. In addition to a bosket crossed by radial paths, an aviary, a maze and a special kind of watery joke can be found: fine jets concealed in small channels forming the shape of the monogram of the House of Orange-Nassau suddenly spray the unsuspecting visitor with water.

The grounds in around 1700
After a coloured engraving by Petrus Schenk

FOLLOWING DOUBLE PAGE:
View of the garden with the Fountain of Venus in the centre and the King's Fountain and colonnades behind.

ABOVE:
View of the lower garden and palace

BELOW:
Sculptural group with colonnades behind

OPPOSITE:
Fountain of Venus

130

Royal Gardens at
HERRENHAUSEN
Hanover · Germany

The history of the Herrenhausen Royal Gardens began in 1666 when Johann Friedrich von Calenberg had a "summer residence with a small garden" built. He named it Herrenhausen. When Duchess Sophie, later electoral princess, chose the (now enlarged) country house to be the summer residence of the House of Hanover in 1680, she effectively laid the foundation stone of Herrenhausen's garden architecture.

In accordance with contemporary ideas, all further plans for the enlargement and alteration of Herrenhausen were intended to make the garden the social centre of the royal court. At the same time Sophie was able to make Herrenhausen a place of rest and relaxation. With her many talents and far-sighted ideas, Sophie was the driving force behind all the landscaping activities at Herrenhausen. In 1682 she engaged the Frenchman Martin Charbonnier as royal gardener, in order to match the very high standards of garden design then being pioneered in France. Charbonnier's Baroque style characterizes the garden to this day.

But France, and in particular Versailles, was not the only model for Herrenhausen. Before the work of extensive renovation and rebuilding was started in 1692, Sophie sent Charbonnier to the Netherlands to study garden design there. She had spent the major part of her youth at the Orange court and hence wanted to see some aspects of Dutch garden design employed in Hanover. The "Graft" built in 1696, a horse-shoe-shaped moat around the sides of the grounds, shows a marked Dutch influence.

The first conservatory was erected in 1686. A further attraction was added in 1689 in the form of a garden theatre. Its stage was 50 metres deep, had a backdrop of reinforced hornbeam hedges and was framed by

Flower parterre decorated with sculptures

gilded lead figures. The auditorium was in the shape of a small amphitheatre, and lay right next to the so-called King's Bush, an articulated area of hedge which served as a kind of foyer. The Baroque garden theatre at Herrenhausen is the only one of its kind which is still used for performances today.

In 1699 the entire south half of the garden underwent homogeneous

Overall view of the grounds
Engraving by J. van Sassen, around 1700

overall restructuring. The layout of the paths was changed so that "triangles" were created from the four square areas which composed the garden; these were then planted with fruit trees and enclosed by beech hedges. This was the *Nouveau Jardin*. Both to the west and to the east of this area, next to the moat, are two semicircular areas. Charbonnier gave these their compositional counterpart in the larger circular area to the south of the garden, the "full moon". Its focal point is a large pool with a fountain at its heart, whose 80-metre high jet of water makes it the highest garden fountain in Europe.

After Sophie's death in 1714 the renovation and restructuring work slowed down, but it never came to a complete standstill. The number of orange trees grew to such an extent that there was no longer room for them in the existing gallery, and so an orangery was built in 1720. By 1727 it contained around 600 orange trees.

A library pavilion was added in 1816. In 1818 more land was purchased, and the Georgian garden was created. In 1845 a mausoleum was built to be the final resting place of the Hanoverian regents.

The Herrenhausen gardens were badly damaged during the Second World War. They were robbed above all of their architectural point of reference: the palace was destroyed by bombs and never rebuilt. Nevertheless, thanks to extensive restoration work, Herrenhausen remains one of the best-preserved Baroque gardens in Europe.

FOLLOWING DOUBLE PAGE:
Bell fountain, surrounded by four
rectangular parterres

133

The Great Fountain

Temple by Remy de la Fosse

Gardens of Schloss
CHARLOTTENBURG
Berlin · Germany

Charlottenburg or Lietzenburg as it was originally called after the town of Lietzow, was planned as the summer residence of Sophie Charlotte (1668–1705), the second wife of King Frederick I. Originally planned as a "simple" country house, it grew over a period of more than a century into a monumental complex and became one of the most important courts in Europe. The palace grounds have a no less illustrious history.

The building of a summer villa with no outhouses was begun in 1695. Designed by Arnold Nehring, its style was simple, even austere. Today, this original building forms the prominent central tract of the palace.

Since gardens played such a major role as the central meeting-place of the court, it was not surprising that Sophie Charlotte herself took charge of the planning of the Charlottenburg estate. With the help of a relation, Liselotte of Orléans, she managed to secure the services of a pupil of Le Nôtre, Siméon Godeau. Godeau's stamp is still evident in the gardens today, although a Dutch influence is also clearly visible. Under Godeau's direction, and with the help of René Dahuron, another garden designer who had worked at Versailles, the most splendid park in Brandenburg came into being within a relatively short time.

The view from the central rooms of the palace overlooked extensive, richly-patterned *parterre de broderies*, which led the eye across a large basin to the River Spree. An avenue across the Jungfernheide heath on the far bank was intended to continue the perspective. While four-row avenues articulated the area between the palace and the course of the river, to the west a geometrical hedge section lay half-way between the palace and a piece of land with straight canals running through it.

View from the palace over the garden

At the same time as the garden was being developed, plans were also put into action to extend the castle. A long wing was erected which sought to integrate Nehring's original building as its centre. Side wings on which work had been begun previously were now connected to the main building forming a broad courtyard of honour. To offer the park a complementary architectural reference point, the part of the palace complex overlooking

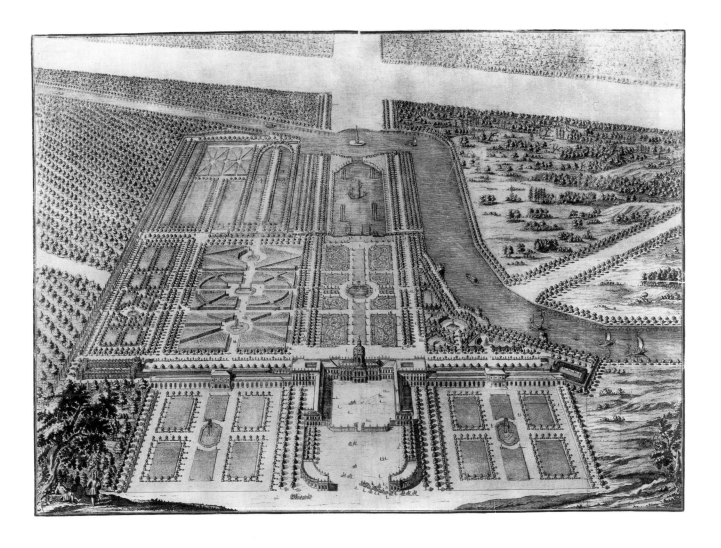

the garden was given symmetrical extensions taking it to three times its former length.

Building work was continued even after Sophie Charlotte's death. Frederick I tried to increase the splendour of his property with ever more projects. Thus the dome and the west orangery were completed in 1712. Frederick did not live to see his plans completed, however. He died in 1713. His successor, Frederick William I, thought it advisable to follow the years of huge expenditure with a period of strict economy. For the time being, expansion and alteration work was stopped. When Frederick the Great took power in 1740, he made the palace his royal residence.

Between 1786 and 1833 the Baroque garden was much altered, this time taking the "English" garden as its model; the ideal garden was now an imitation of nature with waterfalls, ponds, winding footpaths, "natural" clusters of trees and meadows. Three of the garden's chief attractions date back to this period: the Belvedere, the Schinkel pavilion and the mausoleum. The landscape garden was the work of three gardeners, Johann August Eyserbeck, George Steiner and Peter Josef Lenné under Kings Frederick William II and III. The death in 1861 of Frederick William IV, the last king to live in Charlottenburg, heralded the onset of the garden's decline.

The aim of the restoration work which is being carried out today is to come as close as possible to the original wealth of experiences offered by the garden and to the ideas of its designers.

ABOVE AND OPPOSITE PAGE:
Garden front of the palace complex by
Arnold Nering and Eosander von Göthe

ABOVE:
Rows of trees line the spacious gardens,
with their fountain and *parterres de broderies*,
in front of the palace

Mausoleum by Heinrich Gentz
and Karl Friedrich Schinkel

Belvedere
by Carl Gotthard Langhans

Court Gardens at
VEITSHÖCHHEIM
Veitshöchheim · Germany

The origins of the park at Veitshöchheim date back to the 17th century. Between 1680 and 1682 at the behest of the Prince-Bishop of Würzburg, Peter Philipp von Dernbach, a summer residence was erected which was to be the nucleus of the palace later built on the same spot. At the same time, an elongated orchard was planted somewhat to the north. Peter Philipp's successor, Prince-Bishop Johann Gottfried von Guttenberg, sold part of the grounds, giving the garden the boundaries it has today.

Veitshöchheim is considered *the* Rococo garden in Germany, not because of the way the grounds were laid out but because of its large collection of sculptures by Ferdinand Tietz, whose figures vividly convey the *joie de vivre*, the sensuousness and the playfulness of the age. The basic form of the grounds was laid out in 1702–1703 under Prince-Bishop Johann von Greifenclau; they acquired their final form between 1763 and 1776 under the charge of Prince-Bishop Adam Friedrich von Seinsheim.

The entire complex is divided roughly into two areas: the palace area and the pleasance proper, which is in turn subdivided into three, or rather four, regions. Two major axes running parallel but independent of each other form the central lines of reference, not only in the pleasance but also in the area around the palace. A total of twelve parterre gardens laid

out symmetrically around the central axis on an almost square plateau surround the palace. To the south of this area a pathway leads down a flight of steps to the pleasance. Three major regions can here be identified, their boundaries clearly marked by two avenues set at right angles to the central axis.

The largest of the three regions, that around the Great Lake, is quite clearly dominant. Parnassus rises from its waters, together with Apollo and the nine muses and the winged horse Pegasus. At the very centre of the lake, Parnassus is also a point of reference for the perspective continuation of the main axis of this part of the garden, which appears to cut through the waters of the lake before resuming its path on the opposite

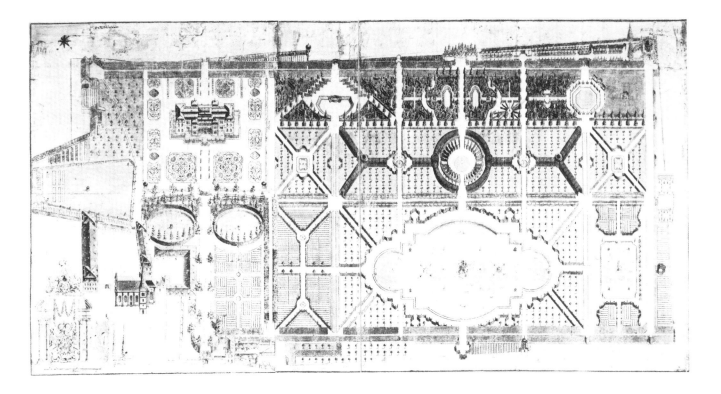

Perspective plan
by Johann Anton Oth, 1780

shore. In Greek mythology Parnassus was the starting point of a new world order under the rule of the Olympian gods. Thus figures representing the gods of Olympus, together with allegories of the four seasons, surround the lake. To the south, a much smaller lake adjoins the Great Lake. The hedge areas surrounding the lake are subdivided by paths running crosswise and diagonally, with fruit and nut-trees filling the spaces in between.

An avenue of lime trees separates the lake from the pergola region. This narrow middle zone contains the heart of the pleasance: the so-called "circus". This circular area ringed by a pergola and bordered by hedges is also dissected symmetrically by the main axis. Two pergolas (today replaced by hornbeams) running parallel to the two avenues lead both in a northerly and in a southerly direction to small hedged galleries and two latticed pavilions. Here the pergolas fork, each following its own path to the edge of the avenues. Two hedge chambers border the middle zone at its narrow ends.

An avenue of spruces forms the border between the pergola and wooded regions. This latter, the third of the three main regions of the pleasance, is further subdivided into three parts: the hedge theatre to the north, the chambers of hedges and lime trees to the south and, in the middle, an area of lawns and fountains.

Groups of figures sculpted by Tietz – mainly putti – stand in both the garden theatre and in the south chamber of hedges. Two basin-shaped sunken springs lie on both sides of the main axis. Here, groups of figures depict scenes from Aesop's fable "The fox and the stork". The style of the sculptures corresponds to that of the nearby Chinese pavilion, where four stone palm trees support a tent-like roof, topped by a leafy crown and with four pineapples capping its pillars. Within the pavilion a stone table and four stone stools are an invitation to stop and rest awhile.

The fourth region of the pleasance is a long, hedge-lined triangle of secondary significance. The perspective of the central axis ends here, terminating in a cascade which has unfortunately been destroyed. From here one has a clear view over to the Great Lake, with Pegasus rearing.

The mount of the muses, Parnassus, in the Great Lake

Hedge with sculptures and the main palace façade

Chinese pavilion in the wooded region

One of the many sculptures by Ferdinand Tietz

Hedge gallery and pavilion

OPPOSITE PAGE:
Grotto house and Belvedere
on the south-east edge of the garden

Gardens of Schloss
SCHWETZINGEN
Schwetzingen · Germany

The history of Schwetzingen palace and grounds can be traced back to the Middle Ages. Old documents and charters prove that as early as 1350 a moated castle stood on this very spot, dominating the neighbouring landscape. This fortress was extensively altered and expanded over the following centuries. In the 16th century it was converted into a hunting lodge. In the 17th century more extensive building work was undertaken in order to give it both the form and function of a summer palace, in accordance with the more sophisticated demands of courtly society. A larger garden was an essential part of these demands. Unfortunately, much of what was built was destroyed by war within the century.

This piece of ground, so laden with history, was re-designed in the 18th century, mainly during the reign of Prince Elector Karl Theodor. The art-loving monarch planned to give the palace and its grounds, now promoted to summer residence of the royal Palatine court at Mannheim, an architectural exterior to match its social position. To ensure the appropriate magnificence of the result, "architectural treasures" were to be created which would take their place within one of the most beautiful gardens in Europe. Karl Theodor appointed such outstanding European artists as Pieter Antoon Verschaffelt and Nicolas de Pigage.

The plans for a new palace built on a larger scale were never realized, but the design of the garden set the standards for the age.

In 1748 Karl Theodor had the central part of the garden, which had been laid out between 1721 and 1734 according to plans by his predecessor Karl Philipp, completely redesigned in the spirit of French garden architecture. The fundamental principle of the Baroque garden, with its expansiveness and its "absolute" order drawn up with a ruler on a drawing-board, was now put into practice in a pure, unadulterated form.

The observer can best appreciate the geometrical expanse of the gardens by walking through the central, fortified-style palace building, with its massive square stone blocks and its gates with their pointed gothic arches, and coming face to face with the system of lines of reference formed by natural objects. Fountains and small waterworks are embedded in the grassy lawns which drop in terraces to the west, their perspective central axis flanked by Dutch lime trees. The Arion Fountain forms the central point of two intersecting, three-lane avenues. The fountain, which was created by Barthélemy Guibal, a sculptor from Lorraine, lies at the centre of an enormous circle which encloses the entire parterre garden. The edge of this circle is determined by two curving buildings right next to the palace; the one to the north was built in 1749–50 as an orangery, while that to the south was erected in 1753–54 to house festivities. Their architectural counterparts are the two treillages erected in the west of the area, which complete the circle. The optical gaps between these four constructions form the starting points of the two avenues. No other Baroque garden has such an original circle – it is only fitting that this one lies at the very heart of the Schwetzingen gardens.

In 1762 renewed extension of the grounds was begun, boskets were planted to the west and the north-west, and a garden of orange trees created. The main axis was extended, thus creating an uninterrupted view through to the Great Lake. The park was also provided with additional buildings and sculptures. An artificial hill crowned by a Temple of Apollo was constructed close to the garden theatre built by Pigage in 1752.

Further to the north, the Bathhouse fits well into the landscape. Also

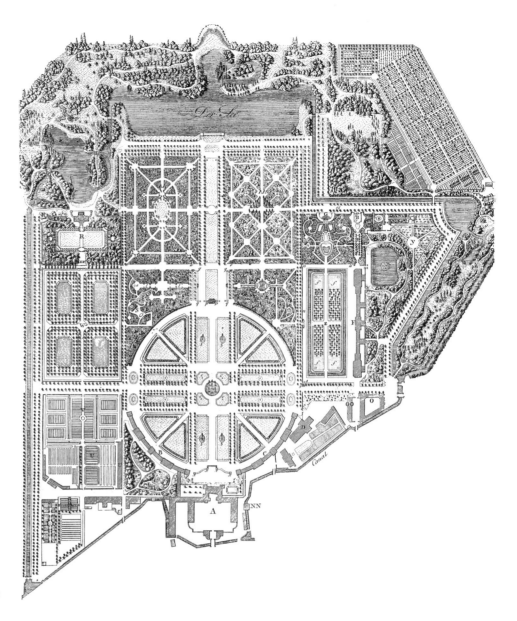

Schwetzingen
after J. M. Zeyher, 1809

designed by the Rococo architect Pigage, it is today considered to be the most valuable building in Schwetzingen's gardens. Two semicircular entrance halls flank a splendidly furnished central room, elliptical in form and with a domed roof. Directly adjoining the Bathhouse is the Bower of the water-spouting birds.

In 1777 the garden architect Ludwig von Sckell was given the opportunity to completely redesign the hilly area at the north and west edges of the garden in the latest style of the English landscape garden. While the geometrical part of the garden remained unchanged, winding paths and waterfalls here meander round "natural" clusters of trees. The bank of the Great Lake, from the centre of which Verschaffelt's depictions of the gods of the Rhine and Danube rivers rise up, lost its regularity. A canal flows into the lake, crossed by the "Chinese bridge" which was once intended to convey an illusion of the exotic.

In 1780 the final part of the grounds came into being: the Turkish Garden, in which can be found what is probably the most original architectural creation in the park: a mosque. With the erection of this building, Karl Theodor fulfilled his intention of giving his park, which was already famous, a unique finishing touch.

Temple of Mercury

OPPOSITE PAGE:
View of the Temple of Apollo

FOLLOWING DOUBLE PAGE:
View over the Small Lake to the mosque

Pergola

Bower with water-spouting birds

III. The geometry of the Absolute

The French Renaissance garden developed initially out of its own mediaeval tradition, with the distinguishing characteristics of the castle and fortress being preserved into the 17th century. But the radical change that took place in garden design in Italy in around – although not before – 1500 can be identified particularly clearly from the Italian influence on French châteaux, from Amboise, Blois and Villandry to Fontainebleau and Dampierre. Both Louis XII and Francis I attached great importance to establishing the new Italian art in their native land. Famous architects were employed, along with the best painters and sculptors from Florence and Rome, and the spacious rooms which resulted were decorated with Italian art. None of the gardens which were laid out at that time attained the design quality of their Italian models, however. Nor shall we be examining why. But epigons of all kinds can be characterized in terms of two revealing aspects: the dominance of intentionality and the presence – often latent, even *malgré soi* – of authentic essence. It is precisely because the 16th century in France was - as far as garden design was concerned – so strongly characterized by transition and self-discovery that the stimuli received and the transformations they underwent can be so clearly distinguished.

The most important parallel with Italy lies in the fact that the French garden similarly did not develop out of the countryside. Its layout was "artful" in every respect, its conception subject to strict rules. Its interior was to be clearly delimited and its design clear and easily comprehensible at all times. The preferred forms of expression were square ornamental beds, strictly-ordered pathways and rows of trees. The demarcation of the grounds from the outside, which for the Italians demonstrated the moment of particularity and individuality, is emphatically signalled in the high walls and towers of French Renaissance châteaux. The French found designing the inner integrity of château and grounds a great deal harder. The terraced architecture introduced by Bramante and so brilliantly developed by Ligorio remained alien to them. They had their own answer to the internal structuring of space: the *parterre*. This will be examined in more detail later on. The gardens of the Renaissance make only trial use of this new spatial concept. Looking back to this first phase from the viewpoint of the highly-developed Baroque gardens of Vaux-le-Vicomte and Versailles, however, it is clear that the French operated with a different, very personal principle right from the start.

The fact that French estates retained their fortress character for such a long time shows that the idea of the unit was understood only in the mediaeval sense of self-withdrawal, and not as a concept requiring universally new design.

Although, at Amboise, the garden was designed in the Italian manner by a Neopolitan architect, Pacello da Mercogliano, on a specially-extended, higher terrace behind the château, it nevertheless remains a separate entity, surrounded by a gallery. It does not succeed in fusing with the château buildings, or even with the garden of orange trees which is laid out to the south. It is like an exotic, precious jewel whose only function is to be admired from all sides.

Pacello also did much of the garden planning at Blois. Here, the lack of interest in the idea of terracing is perhaps even clearer – despite the fact that terraces are present. Three large gardens were laid out on different

Gardens of Schloss *Weikersheim*, Weikersheim, Germany

Perspective view from the castle along the main axis with the grotto mount (centre) through the two-part orangery and on into the surrounding countryside

165

The Gloriette in *Schönbrunn* palace gardens, Vienna, Austria

This colonnaded building in the classical style of the late Baroque was built as a memorial to the successful battle against Frederick the Great near Kolin in 1757 (during the Seven Years War). It forms the uppermost end of the main axis of the grounds; from this point the observer has a splendid view over the gardens, the city of Vienna and its surroundings.

levels. The terraces had to be substantially underpinned, just as at the Villa d'Este. But the architect then made each level a sealed entity. There is no connection of any sort – no steps, no ramps, no passageways. Each part remains separate unto itself, enclosed within high walls. The overall relationship between garden and château is even more problematic. The gardens are separated from the château by a moat and can only be reached by crossing a bridge. It seems that there was never any intention of integrating the two parts or even of creating a state of architectural tension between them. Bury is seen as a first attempt to combine previously merely neighbouring parts into a whole. But even here, the relationship between the four courtyards is simply one of juxtaposition. The architect's real interest lay in the highly artistic design of the eight ornamental beds which embellish the garden behind the manor house. There are no such ornamental beds in the courtyard of honour, which simply features four large lawns.

To this period also belongs the design of a villa which has been attributed to the elderly Leonardo da Vinci. It is a useful illustration of the fact that Leonardo – like Raphael – hat not yet taken the final step towards the modern age's idea of individuality. The plans for the villa, which were made between 1516 and 1519, are undoubtedly influenced by the spirit of classical antiquity. But the design of the villa with its corner towers and moat and the alignment of its individual parts – house, courtyard, garden and pool – remain trapped in the mediaeval world of Dante, which knew order and hierarchy but was still unable to conceive of a process-

bound whole. The French really only came closer to the new Italian style of garden design at the beginning of the 17th century, with the building of the gardens at Saint-Germain-en-Laye and the Jardin de Luxembourg. Marie de'Medici, wife of Henry IV, was the driving force behind their creation. She employed Francini and other Italian artists to ensure that the Italian spirit of the Palazzo Pitti, Ammanati and the Boboli gardens would be copied as authentically as possible in France. A closer look at the results of these huge efforts reveals a striking fact: the adaption and updating of Italian models led to a significant departure from the Italian style and the discovery of a unique French style.

This move can be detected in external elements alone. The French garden aims at *expanse*. It does not wish for firmly-demarcated singularity or individuality. It seeks instead to integrate a *multiplicity* of different features, interrelated via artistic patterns. The difference between "terrace" and "parterre" mentioned earlier becomes evident in Saint-Germain-en-Laye. While Italian terraced architecture is tripartite by nature, the idea of the parterre allows for – one could say almost unlimited – multiplicity. What in Italy was interrelated by tension and fundamental difference is in France diluted into the gentle gradations and nuances of different levels of terrain. Large and small flights of steps, ramps, arcades, fountains, straight and winding covered ways are to be found throughout the grounds at Saint-Germain. Italian architecture seems to have gained acceptance everywhere. Nor is this in dispute. And yet an essentially new conception

The Imperial Summer Residence *Schönbrunn*, Vienna, Austria

It was originally intended to build the summer residence – whose architecture was to surpass in splendour that of all previous castles – on the Schönbrunn hill where the Gloriette now stands. This hill, with its view over the capital of the Empire, seemed the most appropriate setting for the seat of the future "German Sun King". However, partly due to financial reasons, a rather more "modest" plan was carried out in the valley. The palace was designed by the great Baroque architect, Fischer von Erlach.

167

Wall of hedge with sculpture in the grounds of *Schönbrunn*, Vienna, Austria

of space and garden already suggests itself. It is no longer possible to distinguish a polarity between "mind" and "nature", since there is no longer a distinct, absolute "above" and "below". There is no part of the garden which deserves to be described as more or less "art" or more or less "nature" than any other – although the related architectural problems are definitely still discernible. To summarize the difference from a philosophical point of view, it can be said that the *particularity* which characterized the middle zone of the Belvedere courtyard and the Villa d'Este has become the main aim of the whole garden. Its architecture is thus a never-ending process with neither a beginning nor an end, a pathway that comes from somewhere and leads somewhere else. There may perhaps still be "boundaries", whether they be walls, hedges, a river or a roadway; but when viewed from changing points of view they give the impression of being arbitrary, movable, and without any true limiting power. There may even be "peaks" along the way, such as the château, which at Saint-Germain lies very centrally, while standing on the periphery in the Jardin de Luxembourg. But even peaks do not break the continuity of line. They are themselves integrated into the rising and falling course of "events" in the landscape.

This change of orientation had many consequences which only developed gradually in French garden architecture. For Versailles and Louis XIV, probably most important was the shifting of the *time axis*. Ligorio had incorporated the idea of time into the whole by having it countercheck

space in the form of the history of the House of d'Este. The result was a temporal standstill which was expressed in the form of allegory and symbolism. In the case of French gardens, time increasingly attained the position of main axis and from then on ran parallel to space. The effect of this very soon become apparent. What in the Renaissance gardens had seemed so scattered and disarrayed, seemingly obedient to the laws of chance, suddenly fell into harmonious order like pearls on a necklace. In place of stasis there was flow. The act of walking through such a garden itself gradually took on a dimension of time, which was revealed as a structuring and ordering principle.

The *parterre de broderies* have rightly been compared to artistically-choreographed dance figures. Music – as time counted – is part of dancing. Time in the form of music becomes a self-embedding in cosmic dissonance and harmony. It is thus not difficult to imagine the enormous success enjoyed by Jean Baptiste Lully at the court of Louis XIV with the musical entertainments with which he filled the entire park with music. In addition to music, sculpture also fell increasingly under the spell of time. The clever positioning of allegorical figures turned complete parterres into steps in time, views form changing perspectives into the unfolding course of a day or year and a stroll in the park into a journey through the distant realms of astrology and mythology.

The situation with regard to *space* was not much different. The garden became a microcosm in which "nature" and "the world" were portrayed

Grotto in the gardens at *Hellbrunn*, Salzburg, Austria

in successive stages. It was no longer sufficient to set out solitary river gods, nymphs or emblematic allegories. A garden architect was expected to devise a complete programme, a sort of universal philosophy in which the most significant elements had a particular order, followed a logical development and, from meaningful stopping points, guaranteed an overview of the major relationships between mythology and nature. Since *particularity* knows no clear boundary, transitions become all-important. The visitor must always be able to tell what level of the garden he is on, when and how he is moving to another one, and whether he is thereby acquiring more or less in terms of space and understanding – and he must always be able to retain a sense of the garden as a whole. This means that he must be able to look both forward and backward, to anticipate his thoughts and actions as well as bring them into line with what lies behind him, and he should if possible never be surprised by the unpredictable. The inscrutability which characterized the *particularity* of the Italian garden, Ariosto's world of dragons and magic, has been largely domesticated. This is not to say, however, that the French garden is an exercise in superficiality. Quite the opposite: Ariosto's "madness" is changed and intensified in the hands of Corneille and Racine into a tragic awareness of life. While Molière's comedies sprang from the world of Paris and bourgeois city life, the French Baroque garden became the ideal backdrop for the *tragédie classique*. In the works of Racine, too, the dreadful, the sudden, the unforeseen are never shown openly. This does not mean such things never happen, however, nor make his heroes any less tragic for knowing very well how easily the wrong step can lead to ruin and death.

It was not until the second half of the 17th century that André Le Nôtre was able to do justice to the extremely complex, multilayered and subtle idea of particularity with all the necessary *délicatesse*. His first masterpiece was Vaux-le-Vicomte. The story of its owner, Nicolas Fouquet – his success, his boundless wealth, his hubris and sudden fall from grace – reads like a classical tragedy even today. And perhaps there really is an internal relationship between Fouquet and the whole architectural atmosphere at Vaux-le-Vicomte, which succeeded like no other in giving expression to the Baroque sentiment of *vanitas*. No engraving, no overall view or even photograph can capture Vaux-le-Vicomte's "secret", if one may call it that. It can only be experienced by the visitor in person. The decisive question, already answered by the Italians in their own way, is here raised within a few steps of entering the grounds: what and where is nature? In the works of Bramante and Ligorio, the idea of nature, "body" and "physis" were clearly represented by the lower level, the basis of the terraced garden. Every further level could base itself upon this first, either as antipode or intermediary. Le Nôtre had a completely different answer to the question, distinguishing himself once and for all from the Italian architectural style. The garden was to be absolved of the necessity of such a primary level. There was no longer any point of reference, no basis which might be called a "natural foundation" and from which everything else acquired its relative significance.

Even the first impression of Le Nôtre's new way of using space is confusing. The château is surrounded by a moat. At first one is tempted to say that the level of its water is a natural elevation. But one very quickly comes across other areas of water which clearly lie at different elevations but are nevertheless just as natural and self-contained as the moat. A

second approach is to take the house as the zero level of the estate. But compared with the forecourt and the pathway around it, it appears to have been artificially raised, particularly since it sits on a decidedly plinth-like bottom storey. Looking back towards the château from the lower-lying parterres, it certainly appears as an important point of reference; to accept it as a ground level as prespecified by "nature" is, however, less easy. As one proceeds through the garden, one discovers that the dimensions of the individual levels and the height differences between them have been so precisely calculated that one always has a sense of standing on the floor of nature, even down by the canal; and yet this physical certainty is constantly refuted by the evidence of one's eyes. That physical evidence can deceive is most spectacularly proven when, on the path through the parterres to the canal, one turns round and is forced to see how the stairways of the middle axis, which one has gradually descended via the different levels, have – behind one's back – aligned themselves into a single flight of steps. They now lead directly from wherever one happens to be standing up to the great double doors of the Oval Salon. Through this so carefully constructed arrangement, the dimension of space becomes a constantly-shifting variable: areas and distance do not exist because they "are"; by favourably calculating one's position within the continuum of space, they "can" come into being – but they can just as easily disappear again if one changes one's direction or perspective too abruptly.

Thus the idea of *particularity* found its own, completely independent

Vaux-le-Vicomte, Melun, France
Ornamental box hedges in the parterre region

FOLLOWING DOUBLE PAGE:
The Hermitage, Bayreuth, Germany
Lower grotto with fountain group

171

form for the first time. Taking this to its logical conclusion, the dangers of Ariosto's realm of magic appear as still thoroughly conquerable tangibilities. At Vaux-le-Vicomte, Le Nôtre set the scene for something many times more dangerous: the total loss of reality. At every point of his garden design one must reckon with the possibility of the ground – on which one stood so firmly just a moment before – suddenly vanishing. There is no depending on nature as nature. The world is no longer Arcadia, nor even a cushion, but a "stinking sack of maggots" harbouring decay. Le Nôtre managed to grasp the tragedy of the new idea in all its dimensions. It is not the individual, not Orlando who succumbs to madness. "Vain delusion" and "futility" hold sway throughout the whole world. Andreas Gryphius wrote his Vanitas Odes just a few years before Vaux-le Vicomte was built:

> The glory of the earth
> Must turn to smoke and ashes
> No rock, no stone can stand.
> That which can delight us
> That which we prize eternally
> will vanish like a dream.
>
> For what are all things
> Which make our hearts light
> But wretched vanity?
> What is the life of man
> That he must ever drift
> But time's illusion?
>
> The fame for which we strive
> Which we respect so highly
> Is only false illusion.
> The spirit once departed,
> And the mouth fallen silent,
> Asks no one what we did here.
> (from: *Vanitas! Vanitatum Vanitas!*)

Nicolas Fouquet experienced the tragic truth of these verses for himself. He was sentenced to life imprisonment just a few weeks after his day of glory, when even a king had envied him. Not only this personal aspect but also the nature of its architecture make Vaux-le-Vicomte a solemn, almost gloomy creation giving almost unparallelled shape to the tragic Baroque attitude to life. But *particularity* displays not just a bleak face, but tends with almost greater intensity towards *generality*, light, indeed even towards eternity. It again fell to André Le Nôtre to create, in Versailles, a unique monument to the overriding need of his age for magnificence and splendour.

There is no doubt that the park of Versailles is the unsurpassed glory of French garden architecture. The story of its creation can, however, be no more our concern here than the structures and architectural principles of the many facets of its overall plan. Our focus is different. If one views the European garden as a designed landscape, in which art reflects its idea in the mode of nature, our conceptual task is to relate the great diversity of observations to the essential moments of ideas, and to permit historicism only where the ideational juxtaposition of the distinct parts is identical with their historical succession. In the case of Versailles, this means finding the point at which the infinite sequence of particularity extends beyond itself to reach a real and permanent conclusion and thus recognizes the principle of the whole series as one capable of setting all its concrete forms in motion. Only in Louis XIV's surroundings could the idea of the garden be receptive to such an idea of the "absolute".

The region of Versailles initially appeared to be far from predestined to house a garden. The Duke of Saint-Simon described the countryside as dreary, infertile and unhealthy. Le Nôtre's efforts were thus undertaken *despite* and to some extent in *defiance* of nature, and not in harmony with any existing, flourishing vegetation. The ground had to be prepared for miles around before any planting or irrigation was possible. In Versailles as in other gardens, "art" and "artificiality" are again at the forefront.

And yet it would seem advisable to look at the idea of nature a little more closely. It is wrong here to use the terminology of the 19th and 20th centuries discussed at the beginning. Since the time of Schelling, "nature" had stood for an objectivity following its own laws which confronts an absolutely distinct subject as a transcendental or ideational quantity. The Romantic had only to go to the woods or – less adventurously – into the garden in order to experience "nature". The garden architect Peter Joseph Lenné fits into this framework. But such abstractions are unthinkable for the 17th century. It is impossible to speak of a direct subjectivity, of one existing a priori, indeed even of "subjectivity" at all. In the philosophy of Decartes – which is often associated with Le Nôtre's garden design – the outside world is not experienced directly as nature but as *res extensa*: an unstable, constantly expanding and hence consuming negative quantity. Saint-Simon's description thus fitted not only Versailles, but the normal state of the external world in general, the *res extensa*. For something like "nature" and, in consequence, knowledge of nature to develop, it must first be created by *res cogitans*, the thinking thing. It should be noted that thought is also a "thing", a "substance". Indeed, this substantiality alone has true "being", which must in turn be carried by thought, in the form of clear and distinct perceptions, into the substances of the external world. In the second half of the century, the distinction between *natura naturans* and *natura naturata* turned up again (cf. Spinoza's Ethics I, 29). The advantage of this pair of terms is that the rational element – thinking as something which judges things from the outside – moves into the background, and nature itself can be experienced as something which is differentiated within. Thus a point in French garden architecture was reached which may be compared with Bramante's decision in the Belvedere courtyard. Nature as an element of the garden reveals itself as an active force, one which itself produces fundamental processes and is insofar free; on the other hand, it also appears as a positive quantity which is determined by necessities and laws and is hence dependent. Thus particularity reaches its real breeding ground, that of *causality*, which must be carefully distinguished from Cartesianism. Nature is no longer a problem of clear and precise recognition but rather a question of self-production and of having been produced. In order to prevent this omnipresent, permanently self-manifesting production of ever new world and ever new life from plunging into the chaos of arbitrariness and the abyss of transitoriness, all phenomena must be strictly interlinked; there must be a

Schloss *Weikersheim*, garden façade,
Weikersheim, Germany

The ancestral seat of the House of
Hohenlohe grew to its present form over a
period of six centuries, from *c.* 1160 to 1760.
The Baroque garden was laid out after 1708
according to plans made by Court gardener
Daniel Matthieu and replaced the previous
Renaissance garden.

concatenatio which ensures that one thing proceeds from another or at
least appears related to another. Garden design fulfils this demand in its
own way and thereby discovers a truth: there must be *geometry*. The
tragic passions of the human soul which Corneille and Racine put on
stage, the continuously-threatened loss of reality as experienced at Vaux-
le-Vicomte, and now the danger of the active *natura naturans* evolving
away from truth and beauty in the direction of destruction – these can
only be combatted by taking the immanent order in man and things and
applying it to the external world. *More geometrico* was how Spinoza
treated his ethics. Le Nôtre constructed the microcosm of Versailles along
the same lines.

If geometry is not simply to appear as an arbitrary, even compulsory
disciplining of nature, the chain of causality requires a first and last link,
or a principle which connects the separate parts in reality. "Finality" and
"immanent efficiency" are thus sought. These problems had already arisen
at Saint-Germain-en-Laye and Vaux-le-Vicomte. The main axis of the
garden served as a guide around which the various parterres, steps, ramps,
fountains and buildings were arranged. But the beginning and end remained
unclear. Even the château was only one part of the linear arrangement
and could not therefore be taken as a guiding principle for the whole. At
Vaux-le-Vicomte, the infiniteness of the linking process was intensified
by the way in which the individual spatial elements could appear and
suddenly disappear again, depending on the perspective from which they

were viewed. Each step of a stairway potentially held a parterre; one simply had to find the right point of view in order to perceive it. The answer is found at Versailles – and is connected with Louis XIV in the same way as was the spatial design of Vaux-le-Vicomte with Fouquet. Pure "particularity", which allows nothing individual and nothing general apart from itself, aspires to the "absolute" and indeed only achieves its purity as a result of this striving. But the absolute may in no respect be equated with the infiniteness of the linking process. It is an autonomous, real and at the same time ideational quantity. Only in such a form can it claim to be the soul and principle of everything that "is". Such an identity of absolute consciousness and ideational reality was still inconceivable for Marie de'Medici and Fouquet. Louis XIV was the first to live and act with the certainty: I am the Absolute. Thus Versailles became the manifestation of absolute substance. Geometry proved to be a suitable medium through which to tie the totality of being, even the most insignificant and distant parts, to its absolute origin. Thus the path of *natura naturans* is clearly related to its *causa finalis*: there is no point within the enormous grounds at Versailles which could not simultaneously be a way back to the ideational centre.

It is worth considering the "Guide to Viewing the Gardens of Versailles" written by Louis himself. This was by no means a mere royal whim. We know from contemporary reports that up to two thousand visitors came to Versailles every day; deserted avenues and contemplative quiet were

Schloss *Weikersheim*, view of the western colonnade of the orangery

The main axis of the garden, lined by many statues, leads from the centre of the castle to the open exedra of the two-part orangery. The optical extension of this line leads out to the surrounding countryside.

Laxenburg, Austria
Bridge over the Schwechat stream and the
Concordia Temple

What was originally a magnificent Baroque
part was transformed under Joseph II
(1780–1790) and Franz I (1792–1835) into an
English landscaped park. This is essentially
the style which can be seen today – with
ponds and watercourses, cascades and
bridges, a grotto and various other examples
of garden architecture.

clearly out of the question. In view of the demand to see and experience
what was then the intellectual and political centre of the world, the Sun
King condescended – to adapt Leibniz' phrase – to point out the "best
of all possible ways" by which it was possible to attain a maximum of
understanding. The goal was not individual pleasure or relaxation, but to
enter into a general plan which contained the promise of coming closer
to the author of the plan and thus to the spiritual centre of the gardens
and, even more, to the power behind pan-European affairs.

On this tour of the park, Louis also led his visitor through the maze.
Once again the difference between French and Italian architecture is made
patently clear. In the Italian garden, the maze played the part of the body
withdrawing into itself, and symbolized danger for all entangled within
it. Such entanglement is impossible at Versailles because its geometrical
principle is known, and because the King sees himself as the representative
of necessity, which rules as the ordering force, above all in mathematics,
but also in the whole of nature. Thus the maze became a brilliant symbol
of *natura naturata*. Louis XIV calmly takes the visitor by the hand and
leads him into the confusion of the maze, but he remains with him to
escort him out again with no trouble at all. A slight attack of dizziness
might be experienced, as symbolized in the statue of Bacchus which stands
directly in front of the exit. But since Bacchus is a god, "intoxication",
"laetitia" and "desire" are also allowed in, as long as they drink at the
source authorized by the gods.

It would be wrong to see these ambitious devices as simply a transparent,

power-political self-portrait of Louis XIV. While the "absolute" separated the King from all that was beneath him, he nevertheless knew himself, despite this absoluteness, to be very much enmeshed in higher contingencies. The Sun King was no sun god. He certainly did not think of himself as *causa sui*, or as nature's creator. In the Baroque world these positions were already firmly taken: in religion stands God supreme, in mythology Apollo and in nature the sun. But Louis XIV is their first and highest representative. In this idea of *representatio* French garden design finds its most appropriate expression. But we should be as careful to avoid a modern-day interpretation of this idea as earlier with the idea of "nature". Louis XIV was no elected member of parliament; he represented neither a people nor a nation. In the 17th century the world did not begin with individual people and certainly not with things, or *res extensa*; nor did free causality in nature offer a solid basis on which a model of representation could be built. On the contrary, the independently active *natura naturans* lives with the danger of squandering reality, of letting it run like water through its fingers and of falling into the abyss of privation. If anything needs representation in a world like this it is the first and true principle of nature, from which everything originates and flourishes. This principle is left to oblivion because of the self-denial of matter. The absolute monarch pits himself against precisely this oblivion by *re-presenting* reason, *natura naturata*, light and *amor dei*, the love of God. It is only the presence of these powers which make the world a well-ordered whole on its way towards a state where all forces act together in peaceful combination. Le Nôtre had to go far back in order to reach this cosmic dimension. That the palace is not the centre of French garden architecture can be seen in Versailles almost more clearly than at Saint-Germain or Vaux-le-Vicomte. Louis refused for many years to incorporate his father's relatively small hunting lodge within the vast scope of the garden design. Even in later years it was only extended and renovated, never torn down and redesigned. The "garden" and "cosmically-included nature" were to be Le Nôtre's central points of reference right from the start. The garden's main axis runs from east to west, a fact which the architect exploited. The rays of the rising sun refract – at the "Grand Lever", as it were – in the golden tips of the courtyard railings as well from the ornaments and the huge coat of arms in the entrance portal. Upon its arrival in the Courtyard of Honour, the sun is immediately greeted by its representative, coming forward in golden splendour to meet it. If there is such a thing as a dialectic of substantiality, then Le Nôtre gave it form in this courtyard at Versailles: he let the sun's representative receive the light of the sun, absorb it in the matter of gold and, in its changed form, offer it back to the sun as a sign of reverence. In this process, art arises precisely on the boundary drawn so ambiguously from double negativity. This may be the reason behind the Baroque love of highly ornate decoration: the more lavish the twirls and flourishes, the more light and splendour they can "represent".

As the sun climbs higher in the sky it reaches the *Marble Courtyard* and a much more significant encounter. The "Grand Lever" is joined by the "Petit Lever", if one may interpret this ceremony in such a "cosmic" fashion. It takes place in the King's bedroom at the centre of the main storey. The lavish daily ceremony of His Majesty's rising from bed is well-known; but we should not forget that it formed only the second and third act of the drama. The primary event and the real start to the day

was the meeting of the sun and its representative, laid out in nature itself and staged by the architect to take place at the very centre of the main axes, at the intersection of the four points of the compass. Le Nôtre arranged this meeting of the two parties so ambivalently that it is hard to distinguish whether the King got up because the sun had arrived to wake him or whether the sun began to shine because the King had got up.

The second important point in the day was the Roi Soleil's going to bed: "le Petit et Grand Coucher". Perhaps this was an even more important moment; Le Nôtre certainly surpassed himself in its design. The *Grand Canal* is one of his most inspired, much praised creations which indeed mirrors *in nuce* the entire philosophy of French garden architecture. It is aligned exactly to the west. With its fleet of pleasure-boats manned by Italian gondoliers, the canal served the court first and foremost as a source of recreation and a backdrop to grand celebrations. But its ideational task, as determined by architecture's cosmic intentions, was to ensure the sun a glittering and worthy exit from the stage of the day. During the late hours of the afternoon, the canal, like a sea of light, reflects the still powerful rays of the sun towards the palace and into the Hall of Mirrors built in 1678. The canal was completed in 1680, and thus – architecturally speaking – these two elements belong together. The idea of representation here reaches its high point. The natural sun, in the form of its reflection by the water, is drawn into the palace by means of the mirrors. The effect of the morning is repeated, but to a greatly intensified degree. Standing before the windows of the Hall of Mirrors, light appears to shine out of

Versailles, France
Large wrought-iron entrance gate with sun emblem

the palace and into the garden and life of the court. Looking from this ambivalent, in-between state of light down to the canal, one gains the impression that the sun has a double in the water which is gradually rising towards the setting natural sun. The later it grows, the closer become these two suns, until at last they set one into the other. This is truly a Grand Coucher. *Water* once again plays the role of the generality dissolving all individuality. This aspect of water is perhaps even more obvious in garden architecture in France than in Italy, since particularity contains the aspect of generality and the way to the Absolute is nothing other than a process of dissolution at higher and higher levels. This process may be clearly seen in the Latona fountain. It stands on the main axis, directly in front of the water parterre, and forms the first visual halt in the royal tour of the park. Its message is normally interpreted in a political fashion: it announces the victory of absolutism. From a mythological point of view, it shows the mother of Apollo, who has taken refuge on the island of Delos in order to give birth to Zeus' son, while the enemies and pursuers goaded into chasing her by Hera have been turned into frogs and other reptiles. It is an almost rhapsodic illustration of the power of the Absolute in the world to reshape negativity and privation.

But the ideational point where the sun sets has even more far-reaching implications. It would have been thoroughly appropriate to burden this moment of approaching night, as in Vaux-le-Vicomte, with the dead-weight architecture of *vanitas*. But Le Nôtre did precisely the opposite. He managed to make the Absolute appear as a dimension which could overcome, indeed even frighten off "natural" death: at the point where the two suns consumed each other, in other words at the point of the tragic identity of nature and art, the carriage of Latona's son, the sun god Phoebus Apollo, rises thunderously out of the water. Supposed sunset is thus transformed into the rising of an immortal sun in the face of which nature and mind, spatial and temporal axes, history and eternal glory merge into one absolute process. In the Fountain of Apollo, Le Nôtre celebrated the triumph of the ageless mythological god hastening to the brotherly aid of his earthly representative.

Versailles, France
Detail of fountain

PAGE 184:
Stowe, Buckinghamshire, England
View from the Greek temple over the Greek valley

English Landscape Gardens

The gardens at Chatsworth embody four centuries of varied garden history. With their different parts and faces between 1570 and the present day they are among the most famous and fascinating in the whole world. Each glorious age has to compete with all the others for supremacy.

The first park at Chatsworth dates back to the 15th and 16th centuries. It included Queen Mary's Bower, which can still be seen today. The bower with its terrace providing a view over the park was constructed in 1570. The first published reference to the garden was in a poem by the philosopher Thomas Hobbes, *Da mirabilibus pecci*, written around 1627 and first published in 1636. The main grounds at Chatsworth were not begun until 1685, however. Like the gardens at Cliveden, Longleat and Boughton, they were strongly influenced by French garden architecture. The formal garden alone measured 120 acres. The country house was completely rebuilt and gardens were laid out on the slope of the valley. George London (*c.* 1650–1714), head royal gardener at Hampton Court and a widely travelled scholar of garden design, also played a decisive part at Chatsworth. Together with Henry Wise he laid out parterres, bowling greens, greenhouses, ponds with fountains (including C. G. Cibber's Sea-horse Fountain) and mile-long hedges and box topiaries. It was a question not of one but of several gardens, all of them differently decorated with sculptures rich in allusion.

Contemporary visitors were particularly impressed by the contrast between the compassed elegance of the gardens and the desolate marshland which surrounded them. Daniel Defoe called the hillside 'a waste and houling wilderness', where one looked down 'from a frightful heighth, and a comfortless, barren . . . and endless moor, into the most delightful

Landscape Garden
CHATSWORTH
Derbyshire · England

Chatsworth, with the formal gardens neighbouring the house
Engraving of 1779

valley, with the most pleasant garden, and most beautiful palace in the world'. That this contrast is not felt with any such force today is due to the work of Capability Brown in the later eighteenth century.

Brown concentrated, after 1750, on transforming the marshland into a landscape park; he also had large sections of the garden ploughed, levelled and re-sown, however. Brown came to Chatsworth in 1760, perhaps a little earlier. His most important contribution here, as later at Blenheim, was to include the river in his landscaping of the park. He achieved this by means of two interventions which, when taken together, produced a "natural" picture. First he dammed the River Derwent with a modest barrier to create a considerably body of water. A neo-Palladian bridge designed by James Paine in 1763 was built over a narrow part of the river. Brown's new, sweeping driveway led over this bridge to the house. Horace Walpole, during a visit to Chatsworth, wrote that the 4th Duke of Devinshire was: ". . . making vast plantations, widening and raising the

The park after improvements by Capability Brown
Engraving of 1786

River, and carrying the park on to the side of it, and levelling a great deal of ground to show the River, under the direction of Brown".

Luckily not all the Baroque elements were destroyed. The essential features of the large Cascade, built by Grillet, one of Le Nôtre's pupils, in 1694 or 1695 in imitation of the "Riviere" in Marly, were preserved. The individual steps of the cascade are of different lengths so that the falling waters generate different sounds. A system of subterranean pipes carries water to the Sea-horse Fountain, then to a fountain in the west garden and from there back to the river. In 1703 Thomas Archer added a fountainhead water temple at the top of the cascade.

In 1826 the 23-year-old Joseph Paxton was made head gardener at Chatsworth and remained there under the 6th Duke of Devonshire until his death in 1858. Under Paxton, Jeffry Wyatville restored a terrace below the west façade of the house. It was only in 1963 that a new, artful parterre was laid out here; it was based on the ground-plan of Lord Burlington's villa at Chiswick.

Paxton also created new watercourses, mainly in the picturesque style, such as Wellington Rock, the Robber Stone Cascade, an aquaduct built as a ruin, the Willow Tree Fountain and the Great Stove square, today a maze. The artistic terracing of his rock gardens became famous, as did the great glass greenhouse: Paxton was the first to get the Amazonian lily to flower. In 1970, not far from Paxton's Conservative Wall, a hothouse for camellias and other exotic blooms, a conservatory was built to house the extensive collection of rare plants.

OPPOSITE PAGE:
View from the older, formal garden near the house
towards the park landscaped
by Capability Brown

Landscape Garden
CASTLE HOWARD
Yorkshire · England

When Charles Howard, 3rd Earl of Carlisle, commissioned Sir John Vanbrugh (1664–1726) to build him a new castle and accompanying gardens in 1699, this – later so famous – Baroque architect from the school of Christopher Wren was completely inexperienced. He had not even a barn to his credit. By the time of his death, 27 years later, the west wing of the huge castle complex was still unfinished, but Vanbrugh had become the greatest architect of the age. In Castle Howard the two ambitious men, who had originally met in the fashionable London Kit-Cat Club, meeting-place of the Whig opposition, created a challenging and revolutionary estate: there was no secular building in the whole kingdom with a larger dome, no other house with such a forest of vases, statues, busts and chimneys on its roofs, and no garden with such delightful miniature architecture as Castle Howard in North Yorkshire.

The signs of the transition from Baroque to classicism are more evident in the garden than in the late Baroque mansion. Although art historical purists might disagree, this is precisely what makes Castle Howard both so delightful and so important. In their different ways the gardens at Castle Howard, Stowe, Cirencester and Studley Royal all lie between the formal tradition of the late 17th century and the subsequent development of the landscape garden. Vanbrugh, George London, Stephen Switzer and even the dilettante Lord Carlisle himself all paved the way for a style which wished above all to be sublime. They went beyond the Baroque discipline of Versailles and Hampton Court. They wanted expansiveness, but not the straight sterility of monotonous axial avenues. They sought

Roman Bridge and castle by John Vanbrugh
Engraving of 1844

to unseat rigid French canons of form without starting a revolution; they wanted to relax but not abandon the rules.

There are many parts of Castle Howard's more than 5,000 rolling acres which herald this change in style. None of these changes is more important from the point of view of the garden historian than the history of the South Parterre. Where the colossal Atlas fountain – souvenir of a World Fair at the end of the 19th century – today stands in the middle of a lawn, there was in 1710 an arrangement of mock architecture, including metre-

high topiaries, obelisks and archways. The experts are still arguing about how much of this first garden was actually realized.

Ray Wood, the little wood to the east of the house, was laid out according to a design by the garden theoretician Stephen Switzer (1682–1745). Its winding pathways and pergolas led to various clearings containing round garden pavilions, fountains and cascades. At the beginning of the 18th century this "natural" stretch of wood must have posed an audacious contrast to Vanburgh's strictly geometric parterre. Switzer nevertheless noted proudly in 1718: "This incomparable Wood is the highest pitch that Natural and Polite Gardening can possibly ever arrive to . . .". Ray Wood is indeed seen as a turning-point in the history of landscape gardening. Today, however, most of the statues have disappeared, and in 1970 Ray Wood was completely altered and turned into a rhododendron wood.

The long, curving terrace walk begins close to the house and runs in a southerly direction, offering splendid views far over the countryside. The pathway runs above an artificial lake with a broad watercourse constructed in 1732–34 and passes several magnificent figures on its way to Vanbrugh's last work, the neo-Palladian Temple of the Four Winds. The most pronounced point of reference is Hawksmoor's colossal mausoleum (1728–29). Daniel Garrett's Roman Bridge is further south down in the valley. Last on the horizon is Hawksmoor's monumental pyramid in the middle of the sweeping pasture-land. Despite some rather clumsy alterations, the general impression of the grounds is still overwhelmingly and incomparably sublime.

Mausoleum by Nicholas Hawksmoor

FOLLOWING DOUBLE PAGE:
Atlas Fountain and Baroque castle complex by Vanbrugh

193

FOLLOWING PAGE:
Temple of the Four Winds, Vanbrugh's last work

Landscape Garden
BLENHEIM
Oxfordshire · England

Sir John Vanbrugh's masterpiece is indisputably Blenheim Palace, begun for the 1st Duke of Marlborough in 1705 following Malborough's defeat of the French at the Battle of Blenheim, in Bavaria. While Vanbrugh's remarkable architecture may be seen as a departure from classical forms, the original gardens by Henry Wise were still heavily indebted to the style of Le Nôtre. Court gardener to Queen Anne, Wise laid out a huge geometrical parterre no less than 31 hectares in size on the hill in front of the palace. To this he added a kitchen garden surrounded by a high brick wall. The parterre was an architectural garden, in which evergreen arabesques of box contrasted with brick dust and marble pebbles. Vanbrugh's second master-stroke at Blenheim was the building of a monumental bridge in the style of Palladio. After Marlborough and his architect had decided on the exact location of the house, it was discovered that a broad, sloping valley lay in the direct path of the drive. The River Glyme and its tributaries ran through the valley, turning part of the ground into swamp. Two raised footpaths and some small bridges had been built across the marsh which were used as short-cuts from Woodstock to Oxford. Vanbrugh wanted to turn the marsh into a decorative element spanned by the most splendid bridge in the whole of Europe. At first the Duke was cautious. He consulted Christopher Wren, who came up with a more modest and less expensive plan. But even the Duchess's criticisms of Vanbrugh's grandiose plans did not prevent him winning the contest, and his huge bridge was indeed built, dwarfing the narrow River Glyme.

Not long after Marlborough's death, his widow asked her chief engineer, Colonel John Armstrong, to redesign the plumbing system. Armstrong had the River Glyme canalized and dammed, producing a lake to the west, where Vanbrugh had also dreamed of making one. The new conduit system came up to expectations and was able to supply the east wing with

John Vanbrugh's masterpiece:
Blenheim Palace
Engraving of 1787

water, but from an aesthetic point of view it was rather a disappointment.

In 1764 the Marlborough family commissioned Lancelot Brown to design the landscape. Within the year he had the parterre levelled and grass sown. In accordance with his principle of "grass to the very door", the meadow now grew right up to the Baroque façade of the palace. Even more astonishing was what Brown did with Vanburgh's bridge and the River Glyme. Except for one very small part – now known as Elizabeth's Island – he got rid of the two driveways, and built a dam and an impressive waterwork on the west side of the bridge. The water flooded the land and formed two large, entwined lakes which came together under the bridge. The piers of the bridge now stood lower in the water, causing the structure to lose some of its visible size and balancing the relationship between bridge and water. The result was a grandiose setting and a break-

Palace and Great Bridge by Vanbrugh
Engraving of 1787

through in garden design. But who was the man who transformed the Baroque Blenheim with such confidence and aggression into a new show-piece of English landscape gardening?

Lancelot Brown (1716–1783), who was later nicknamed "Capability" because his garden designs were always based on the "capabilities" inherent in the landscape, was a pupil of Kent, who summoned him to Stowe in 1741. Brown's characteristic clumps of trees, which are also to be found at Blenheim, were adopted from Kent. In contrast to Pope, Hoare, Shenstone and Lyttleton, Brown was the first professionally-trained gardener to work in the landscape style. By the time of his death he had improved no fewer than 211 gardens, and the transformation of southern and central England into a never-ending park landscape was mainly his doing.

Brown was less interested in classical landscape painting and pastoral literature than in the immediate sensory effect of natural elements. The composition of a sweeping stretch of landscape was more important to him than a series of eloquent garden images. He thought that park and countryside should merge into one another with no visible transition. While he was very economical with his architecture, not one of Brown's gardens lacked a serpentine lake with gently curving, somewhat bare banks. His drives were no longer frontal avenues running up to the main portal, but instead extensive, sweeping approaches which drew up to the house at a tangent. Brown's improvement of an existing region or garden attains, in Blenheim, a magnificent climax.

ABOVE:
The water terrace, viewed from the palace balcony

RIGHT:
Detail of the wrought-iron entrance gate to the palace courtyard.

LEFT:
Palace façade in the evening light, viewed from the lake

FOLLOWING DOUBLE PAGE:
Three views of Brown's lake and park landscape

Landscape Garden
STOWE
Buckinghamshire · England

Stowe, today a boarding school with a golf course, was once an important centre of Country Party opposition to the Hanoverian Kings George I and II.

Lord Cobham (1699–1749), a Whig officer who had played an important part in English victories over Louis XIV but who later fell out of favour at court, gathered around him at Stowe a circle of the young and politically rebellious – known as the Boy Patriots – and engaged the most progressive architects to lay out an extensive garden in keeping with his political and philosophical ideas.

As for the mansion (Vanbrugh), so too a whole series of architects and landscape designers were employed on the plans for the gardens at Stowe, whose style and design were subject to developments and alterations throughout the course of an entire century.

The gardens were begun in the modest and formal style of the late 1680's, but were greatly enlarged in about 1715 and furnished with magnificent buildings and temples. By 1720 Stowe looked as if it intended to compete with Versailles itself.

The garden architect at the time, Charles Bridgeman, was by no means bound exclusively to the magnificence and pomp of formal gardens; he was one of the first in England to take an – albeit cautious – look at landscape gardening. He built a sunken ha-ha wall – so called because of the exclamations of surprise it produced – around the garden, in order to allow better views of the surrounding countryside. Around 1730 Bridgeman was replaced by William Kent, who began to do away with the strictly measured pathways and avenues. To the east of the main axis he created the gently curving Elysian Fields, with their allusion to the after-

Villa mansion by Vanbrugh around 1740

world of the ancient Greeks and as a reminder of the spirit of classical Italy as seen in the paintings of Claude Lorrain or Gaspard Poussin. The stream which ran through this valley was named after one of the rivers of the underworld, the Styx; on its banks Kent built several temples whose reflections shimmer in the waters of the lake. These include the Temple of Ancient Virtue inspired by the Roman sibyl temple at Tivoli. Statues of all the great poets, philosophers, lawgivers and generals of ancient Greece – Homer, Socrates, Lycurgus, Epaminondas – were erected. The Temple of Modern Virtue was built as a ruin, symbolizing the decline in moral standards of the present age. On the opposite bank of the river was the Temple of British Worthies, a semicircular monument in the style of a Roman tomb, with the busts of fourteen British heroes and heroines:

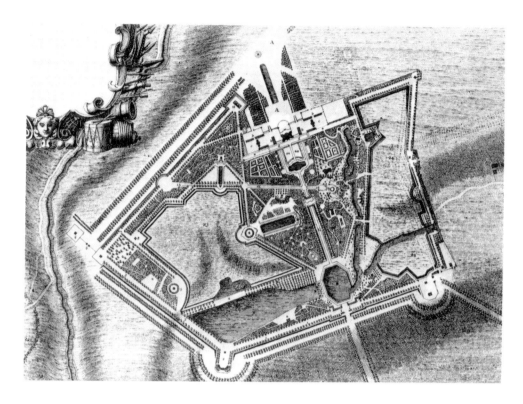

Plan of the grounds around 1740

political figures such as Queen Elizabeth I and King William III of Orange, philosophers Francis Bacon and John Locke, poets William Shakespeare and John Milton, the great Sir Isaac Newton and others. Lord Cobham and his Boy Patriots used to gather in the Temple of Friendship at the end of the Elysian Valley to discuss the overthrow of the Government and the future of the nation.

To the east of the Elysian Fields was a more rugged and "natural" landscape, Hawkwell Field, a rolling, hilly area. There is no point from which the whole of Hawkwell Field can be seen at one time. The Temple of Friendship by James Gibbs (1739) stands in the south; to its north is the Palladian bridge (around 1740), probably also by Gibbs. The bridge is one of the several monumental architectural showpieces of the sort that were soon to become typical of the landscape garden. The bridge at Stowe crosses the eastern arm of an originally octagonal basin whose geometrical shape was softened by Kent. Gibbs' Gothic Temple (1744) stands at the highest point of Hawkwell Field. At first it was called the Saxon Temple, because at the time it was believed that the Saxons had lived as free citizens in contrast to the French under their tyrannical king. Thus the temple was built as a free, irregular shape, with towers of different heights, as a contrast to the regular buildings of France. Gothic was then believed to be the style which best glorified the nation's past.

In 1741 Kent invited Capability Brown to Stowe. As head gardener he played a decisive part in the design of the Grecian Valley, an extensive meadow in the north of the Elysian Fields.

FOLLOWING DOUBLE PAGE:
Lake and park landscape after Brown with Temple and Roman bridge

Palladian bridge over the eastern arm of the lake

Replica of a Roman stone bridge

ABOVE:
Neo-Gothic Saxon Temple
at the top of Hawkwell Field

BELOW:
Landscaped scene after Capability Brown

OPPOSITE PAGE:
Garden front of the mansion by John Vanbrugh

210

Landscape Garden
STOURHEAD
Wiltshire · England

Towards the middle of the 18th century, it became fashionable among the reform-oriented nobility and literati to dabble in garden design. Some of the most influential gardens of this period were designed and laid out by their wealthy owners themselves, albeit sometimes with expert help. They brought back new ideas from their grand tours of the classical seats of learning in Italy which they then endeavoured to transplant onto home ground. Stourhead in Wiltshire is one of the best examples of this English tradition, alongside such as Woburn Farm and Pains Hill in Surrey and the poet William Shenstone's house, The Leasowes.

At the age of thirty-six, Henry Hoare the younger, banker and financier and friend of Alexander Pope, retired almost completely to his father's country seat and began to lay out a garden there. His first design was a central lake with a path around its shores, along which were sprinkled a small number of different temples, each representing a scene from Virgil's *Aeneid*. Hoare's architect was Henry Flitcroft who, as one of Lord Burlington's circle, naturally designed the temples in the Palladian style. A further indication that Hoare himself followed Burlington and Kent's "natural" tendences was his planting of the – entirely altered – landscape with fir and beech. He planted on a large scale, and the originally agricultural flavour of the countryside was soon transformed into a setting of woods and water. The rhododendrons and the arboretum of the present day are later, historically inappropriate additions.

The garden is nevertheless one of the most impressive and best-preserved examples of classical English garden design. The individualistic sense of freedom, a Rousseauesque glorification of nature and the neo-humanist cult of classical antiquity were seldom combined to such effect as in the total work of art that was Stourhead.

View from Diana's Hill towards Hoare's reproduction of a landscape painting

While Kent used the composition methods of landscape painting to construct three-dimensional *vedutas*, Hoare was the first to produce, at Stourhead, a remarkable reproduction of a landscape painting using natural resources. The idealizing pictorial model for this natural garden panorama is thought to be Claude Lorrain's *Aeneas on Delos*. As prototypes of an Arcadian harmony between man and nature, Lorrain's idealized landscapes, with their transfiguring vision of classical antiquity and Mediterranean light, were coveted collector's items in England. Hoare, too, owned

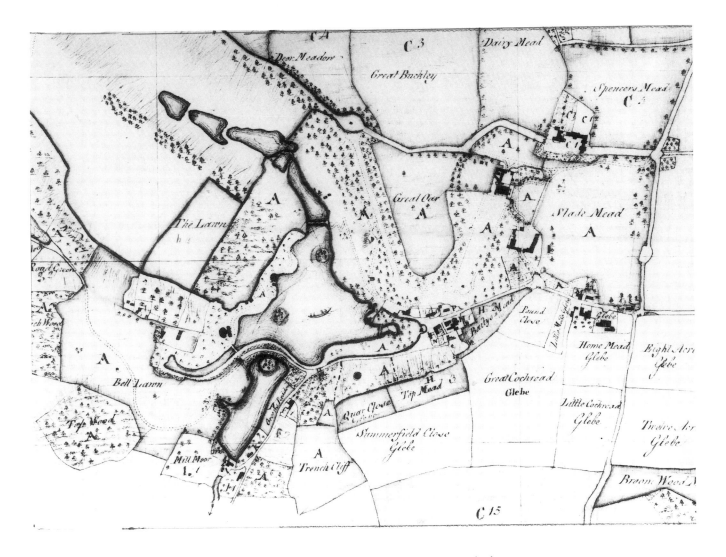

Plan of the grounds, 1785

copies of works by Lorrain. A walk through a landscape garden nevertheless offered the advantage of a sequence of changing park vistas.

Looking across the lake from the village, one beholds a three-dimensional scene of nature which is a conscious reproduction of the classical pastoral landscapes of Claude Lorrain. A small-scale version of the Roman Pantheon, framed by ancient trees and reflected in the waters of the lake, rises between islands on the opposite bank. The Pantheon motif was very popular in classicist parks – Burlington's Chiswick, for instance – since it could be used to convey a multitude of allusions to a suitably educated public: the decline of the Roman empire (with the Pantheon as the only completely preserved temple), its pantheistic background, its cosmological symbolism, and its role as a source of inspiration for Palladio and English neo-Palladianism; it was furthermore linked to Arcadian painting and naturally served as a reminder of personal pilgrimages to Rome in one's youth. The carefully-designed pathway through the grounds to this temple can be understood as the search for the New Rome and an ideal society.

If, on the other hand, one stands directly in front of the monumental architecture of the temple and looks back over the lake, another pastoral picture of the garden presents itself – this time in the English Romantic style. A Palladian stone bridge crosses one of the arms of the lake; behind it is the little village of Stourton – a row of ivy-covered Tudor cottages. Only purists see local scenery as a stylistic incongruity in the Arcadian landscape. It is a testimony to Hoare's vision of rebuilding Arcadia in England.

Neo-Palladian stone bridge
in Roman style

Small-scale copy of the ancient
Roman Pantheon

ABOVE AND BELOW:
Village church and neo-Gothic market cross
at the park exit

OPPOSITE PAGE:
View of the Temple of Apollo

IV. All the world's a stage

In the search for their respective ideas of the garden, in both Italian and French garden architecture the first and most important question concerned "nature". But the answers were not what one might at first have expected. Particularly surprising was the fact that, with the gradual development of the French idea of the garden, it was not only the outer form, the individual elements and their organization that changed; the very concept of nature itself also underwent a fundamental transformation. To the Italians, "nature" within the framework of individuality, as physis and body, as herbal and useful garden, formed the lowest level of the garden; however, it took its ideational reality from its immanent polarity to the "mind" and "art" and from their mediation process, as expressed in the rich and extraordinarily imaginative use of terraces and fountains.

In contrast, French garden design – despite the abilities of artists such as André Le Nôtre – was, from an early stage, criticized as "unnatural". The division of nature into *natura naturans* and *natura naturata* within the framework of the idea of particularity reveals, however, that for Le Nôtre, particularly at Versailles, the theme of nature was one of key importance. The French garden does not employ polarities and thus uses no terraces or confrontative elements. Instead it is interested in the *causality* of natural events, the power of necessity and the force of laws which take effect in nature. It thus traces, *more geometrico*, the long history of the emergence of things back to their absolute origin and at the same time celebrates the work of this absolute origin in all its parts. With its allegorical and mythological symbolism as well, French garden architecture becomes no less than the depiction of nature in all its cosmic, indeed pantheistic breadth.

These distinctions validate the formal premises of our original decision to ban any rigid concepts and *not* to assume that "wood" means "wood" and "nature" means "nature". If one is willing to concede a fundamental reorientation on an ideational level, one becomes sensitive to the fact that the French Baroque garden was also a landscape architecture giving fundamental expression to the idea of nature.

For the English of the 18th century, the question of nature no longer seems problematic, since "nature" was their rallying-cry right from the start, and the banner behind which, within the course of a few decades, they achieved a victory over rationalism and formalism throughout Europe. The English garden has enjoyed unbroken popularity right up to the present day. But even though the idea of nature they express is related closely to that of our own times, it nevertheless remains to be asked whether the landscapes of William Kent and Capability Brown really achieved the immediacy and natural continuity which they claim.

The declared enemy of the English architects was the "formal" garden of French provenance. This hostility was primarily the consequence of English encounters with Italy. William Kent, one of the founding fathers of English garden architecture, studied in Rome; here he met Lord Burlington and the two then travelled widely through Italy. Indeed, a knowledge of Italy was one of the basic qualifications of every educated Englishman, and it was these well-educated young noblemen who, as *dilettanti*, were the first to incorporate their oppositional ideas into the design of new garden landscapes.

Petworth, West Sussex, England
Small temple in the middle of the landscape garden

219

ABOVE AND OPPOSITE PAGE:
Rosendael Park, Arnhem, The Netherlands

These gardens in the Gelderland are characterized by an irregularly-shaped lake and park landscape. The water staircase (above) on the shore of one of the lakes is bordered by two sculptures: are they Mercury and Neptune or allegories of the Rhine and Ijssel?

If one examines the – later highly standardized – *basic canon* of English garden architecture, however, it emerges that its fundamental laws not only have very little to do with the Italian ideas of the garden, but that they even contradict it:

1. The Italians made substantial use of "terraces" to structure their gardens. The English rejection of the French "parterre" did not mean a return to pronounced terracing, but on the contrary to a clear ban on terraces. The landscape was to be *hilly*, without abrupt interruptions or edges, without angles or plumblines.

2. There were to be no more main or lateral axes dividing the garden into clear, distinguishable compartments. The right angle was frowned upon. Pathways were to "snake" through the countryside. Kent's basic conviction was that "nature abhors the straight line", and William Hogarth went so far in his *Analysis of Beauty* (1745) as to describe the *serpentine* as the line of beauty.

Where – in accordance with these specifications – pathways wind gracefully through hills and dales, there can be no place for the flights of *stairs* or complex *ramps* which the Italians found indispensable as a means of giving their gardens a clear, deliberate structure.

3. *Waterworks* were to be avoided at all costs. This was one of the most important consequences of the new English idea of landscape. Even before the French, the Italians had used water, as a "shaped fluid", to mediate between "nature" and "mind" in a process which we have called the mode of particularity. Fountains symbolized the possibility that the individual parts of inert matter could – through art and intellectual effort – merge into higher unities and that the differences in elevation can be overcome. Since water can portray "development" and "transformation", it can render visible the pneumatic power of the intellect. The banning of water-works makes it quite clear that the enthusiasm of the English for Italy must have been inspired by something other than this central aspect of process-bound mediation.

4. *Parterres de broderies* were replaced by uniform, borderless lawns which if possible come right up to the house. A typical ideal English garden would include neither a *trimmed hedge* nor a *maze*, neither a *fence* nor a *boundary wall* surrounding the grounds.

These decisions can also be viewed as a turning away from the Italian idea of the garden. The boundary was so important to the Italians because they could use it to portray nature as a clearly outlined and individual entity. While the French cultivated the process of particularization, the Italian garden was based entirely on the idea of the peculiar. By examining the treatment of the concept of the boundary in garden architecture we can establish the existence of three basic camps, including that of the English:

– The *clear boundary* makes distinctions, guarantees individuality by excluding everything alien and allows freedom in the sense of independence

both from other individuals and from universal totalities. This boundary simultaneously contains within itself – in the form of the maze – the threat of disaster, and lives in constant danger of physical and spiritual self-consumption.

– The *parterre de broderies* breaks through. It brings individual parts together, the barrier weaving them into intricate patterns of social interaction and enjoying the spiritual dialogue between all its various parts and lines. Holding the whole together is difficult, however, and thus the embroidery parterre becomes the choreography of a form of life which oscillates between a tragic fall and the brilliant attainment of an absolute dimension.

– The *lawn* of the English garden permits neither individual line nor particular dialogue. It signifies the triumph of generality. This generality claims to be the same everywhere: equally present, equally fact, equally inviting and gentle, equally fertile and equally lively. Dangers, the English garden architect would say of his lawn, are unthinkable, indeed out of the question. It is impossible to get lost on a lawn, impossible to feel ill at ease. Since it allows no differences, there can be no injustice. All men are equal on a lawn, be they beggars or kings. From this point of view the lawn is anti-monarchist. To want to read into it the claim to the "absolute", or even the call to "absolutism" and a system of rule whose principle lies beyond the lawn itself, is senseless and backed by no concrete evidence.

With this new idea the English took the final step towards the Enlightenment. This was not merely a modification of garden design but a new

ABOVE AND LEFT:
Rousham, Oxfordshire, England

Rousham, which is mainly the work of the great garden architect William Kent, is considered a virtually perfect example of the English landscape garden of the early 18th century. Kent designed a series of "scenes" – connected by narrow footpaths, but carefully separated from one another – so that the various pavilions, springs and sculptures were presented to the visitor in a well-planned sequence. The different scenes also provide unexpected views over the Oxfordshire countryside.

FOLLOWING DOUBLE PAGE:
Petworth, West Sussex, England
A ruined temple in the garden of Petworth House

223

way of viewing man, his hopes and feelings, the political situation, indeed the whole world. And thus it is particularly valuable to study the claims and the reality of the English idea of the garden more closely. Since it has been shown that the real interest of the English was in "generality", it is perfectly understandable that they were rather sceptical about the Italian concept of nature, which was too much dominated by boundaries, dividing lines and individualism. If there are no higher nor lower levels, then there is no need for any processes of mediation between them. Flights of stairs, ramps and fountains have no meaningful role to play when there is no difference in essence between an open area on a hilltop and a shady grove in the valley below. The English admiration of Italian garden design can be narrowed down to their interest in just one layer of Bramante's terraced architecture: the uppermost level of the Belvedere, the site which commands "beautiful panoramas", "art" in its widest sense, indeed generality.

This is the key to the idea of the English garden landscape and to its position with regard to its two continental predecessors. In no respect does it fall behind the intellectual, art-oriented standards of the Italians or French. On the contrary, it surpasses them many times over because it only accepts that which has generality. This claim to generality means nothing less here than in the two previous cases: "nature" is that which art selects, retains and develops as nature. There is a surprising tendency to overlook the disciplined nature of English artistic dictates and to accept without second thought landscapes which have been designed and laid out according to exact rules as "unbroken" nature. The English landscape garden was, in fact, no less a precisely calculated artificial world than were French and Italian gardens.

Although waterworks were forbidden, this did not mean that no water was allowed at all. It was not, however, to be given its own shape in rectangular pools, oval springs or fountains. Apart from the naturally flowing, uncanalized stream, only one other form of water was permitted: the *lake* as a broad stretch of water with an irregular shore. This irregularity was a binding rule. Capability Brown used the same technique over and over again to create countless lakes, namely by damming usually relatively small streams and by *predetermining* the contours of the lakes which resulted. The concept of "predetermination" is entirely appropriate at this point. Its context is the *Théodicée* which Leibniz first published in Amsterdam in 1710, just a few years before the first of the English landscape gardens came into being at Twickenham, Chiswick and Stowe. Two of Leibniz' themes are particulary relevant to the new conception of nature. The first is that of *contingency*. Leibniz compared the principle of identity, whose truth is founded on mathematical necessity and identical propositions, with a second principle, that of reason. He needed this principle in order not to have to trace the diversity of material objects *more geometrico* to strict laws. There is so much in the world, he argued, which does not exist because it necessarily *must*, but which nevertheless has a *good reason* for why it is there, and for why "it" is there rather than "another". This second kind of existence is thus founded not on identity and law but on choice and freedom. Leibniz called this mode of existence contingency. It is often interpreted as "chance", but this interpretation results from a misunderstanding. Chance has *no reason* and is based on arbitrariness. Contingency on the other hand obeys a principle, the principle of Reason. This principle links the existence of all things which appear arbitrary to

the work of Reason by providing good and plausible reasons for their existence – not by law, but via freedom and choice. The epoch was known as the Age of Reason and its most important representative in England was Alexander Pope. It is surely significant that the poet, who enjoyed huge esteem during his own lifetime, was also – with the design of his Twickenham garden – the founder of the new English style of landscape gardening. We will examine later how he determined the details of the relationship between "Nature" and "Reason".

The second theme concerns generality itself. Man's real "theodicy experience" consists of the fact that it is impossible to experience the world as a whole. One is only ever confronted with fragments and details and must observe how injustices take place everywhere and how power is usually in the wrong hands. To react with doubt and scepticism would be understandable. Theodicy provides an optimistic alternative to this attitude of resignation, claiming that a view of the world which takes the two principles of Reason into consideration must lead to the conclusion that the true ruler of the universe is just and that good outweighs evil in the pre-established general order of things. Theodicy thus opposes outward appearances and calls on mankind to trust the power of Reason.

The lake in the English landscape garden can be interpreted analogously. The still expanse of the lake represents a life-giving unity whose universally pleasant and beneficial effects, while real, are "implied" but never "revealed". Hence the analogy: this general effectiveness may not reveal itself to the individual observer, the strolling visitor. Everything – the winding

Studley Royal, North Yorkshire, England

Studley Royal was the creation of a failed politician: John Aislabie was Chancellor of the Exchequer under the Whigs. Ruinous speculation as chief financier of a South Pacific trading company cost him his office and his reputation. His flight from what he saw as a thankless world became his second career.

The moon lakes in the middle of the extensive grounds are famous. A circular pond in a gentle meadow setting is bordered by two curving ponds, forming a semicircle. The dense wood bordering this broad exedra act as a backdrop giving the whole area the form of an antique theatre. At the vertex of the semicircle, Aislabie built a temple in the classical style which is beautifully reflected in the water.

shores of the lake, the lie of the footpath, the differences in elevation, the trees, the small islands in the middle of the lake – had to be so planned that it was absolutely impossible to view the lake as a whole, no matter where the observer chose to stand. As the theodicean God is self-concealing, so the lake of the English landscape garden was self-denying. And yet it nevertheless had to captivate and convince the observer of its generality. This was achieved by means of the unexpected views which the architect provided for him at every turn. The declared goal was to surprise and astonish the lover of nature and thereby to constantly increase his confidence in the positive powers of nature.

This "religious" moment in the experience of the English garden should not be overlooked. The existence of a preestablished design in the English landscape garden was confirmed particularly clearly by William Shenstone, another dilettante landscape architect. He laid a footpath round the grounds of The Leasowes which followed a sequence of impressive vantage points and inscribed plaques, and he was generally rather annoyed if walkers did not follow his route exactly. This is not too far removed from Louis XIV's guided tour of Versailles. But such prescription of an experience of nature based on freedom and contingency simply reinforces the impression of rigidity and compulsion. The same could be said about the specification of the *serpentine* as the "line of beauty". "Necessity" or "determinacy" is not a quality like "blue" or "liquid" which suits one thing but not another; it is rather a "modality" which arises from use and from its dependence upon a principle. If the serpentine is declared the obligatory line in the garden, its winding nature makes it no less enforced or determined than a straight line or right angle. Mathematical necessity is just as applicable here as to more conventional forms. By the beginning of the 18th century mathematics had already advanced far beyond Euclidean geometry. Differential and integral calculus, in other words the calculation of irregular curves and areas, were the order of the day. The serpentine is strikingly similar to the fall of a classic differential curve with its maximum and minimum. From this point of view the English landscape garden can be seen as a tribute to the mathematics of the age.

Around the turn of the century there was a famous argument between the two philosophers John Locke and Leibniz about whether man's ideas were "inborn" or simply "learned" and therefore external to the mind. As an empiricist, Locke argued the second view by referring to imbecile children who, he said, had no ideas because they learned none. Leibniz sought to prove him wrong with an example from mathematics: when drawing unconnected lines and curves at random on a piece of paper, one normally proceeds from the assumption that pure chance is at work, free from all rules and inner reason. All the greater, therefore, is one's surprise when a geometrician comes along who is able to draw a coordinate system and, after some thought, find a function which describes the exact course of the lines. Hence: even when the formula is not recognized at once, the irregular is still no proof of the absence of reason. The empiricist can thus be countered: even imbecile childen may have inner reason; other people may simply not immediately recognize it.

If one applies to garden architecture the realization that an irregular line is no less geometrical or even rigid than a straight one or a right angle, one must concede that a landscape by Capability Brown is no less "determined" than a parterre by Le Nôtre. The difference is simply that in the

Studley Royal, North Yorkshire, England

Fountains Abbey, the ruins of a 12th-century Cistercian church and cloister, lies in a slight dip on the western edge of the grounds of Studley Royal. Aislabie's son William integrated the Abbey into the gardens in order to give them an additional romantic and picturesque touch.

Mellerstain House, Berwickshire, Scotland

This garden, laid out in 1909, shows that the traditions of the English landscape garden have survived into the present century. Here, too, a formal garden close to the house is closely related to the surrounding landscape – a rarity in Scotland.

case of the French it is the *ruler* drawing a straight line which guarantees discipline, while in England it is a *function*. The ruler establishes clear definitions while the function works with variables and is therefore general. This generality is contained not just in curved lines but equally in the spaces they open up. The lake, the pathways and meadows, the hills and valleys all share the same spirit, so to speak, and at the same time always remain the manifestation of a function. Brown's contemporaries very quickly noticed this constraint and accused him in his landscapes of "schematism". This was unable to damage the persuasive power and success of the serpentine line.

The importance of the idea of generality to the English garden is especially clear in its treatment of the *solitary tree*. From Kent onwards, they populated the broad meadows and stood among the landscape like lonely heroes. The pictorial and picturesque origin of the solitary tree is often traced back to Baroque landscape painting, particularly to the works of Claude Lorrain and Jacob van Ruisdael. But appealing as this theory may be, it does not bear closer scrutiny. There are indeed many single trees and small groves to be found in Lorrain's painting which may have inspired the "clumps" of Brown and Kent. But the idea of a Lorrain picture was very different to that of an English garden. Claude generally painted evening landscapes, where the sun was just setting or had already set in shades of pale yellow. His classical architecture, like the ships returning home and the waiting people, was immersed in the melancholy of transience. Soon night would fall and there would be nothing left. Everything was

enveloped in the darkness of death. Jacob van Ruisdael's painting was not dissimilar. No other Baroque Dutch landscape painter used such sombre colours, dominated by the spirit of *vanitas*. When Claude painted a tree or grove, he generally assigned it to the characters in his titles: *Abraham taking leave of Hagar; Jacob with Laban and his daughters; Aeneas on Delos.* If one recalls what these stories were about, it is impossible to overlook the tragedy inherent in Lorrain's landscapes. Betrayal, disappointment and ruin lie in wait behind his trees, while his architecture tells of a disastrous past and a fateful future.

This tragic principle is completely missing from the English landscape garden. As already indicated, it was conceived specifically to exclude the abyss of individuality and the tragic dangers of particularity. Neither the atrocities to be found in Ariosto nor the fateful happenings in Racine's tragedies could take place in an English garden. The literature which best corresponds to William Kent's gentle hilly landscapes was written by the classical poet, Alexander Pope. But this affinity – confirmed by his garden at Twickenham – is usually overlooked. English garden design is more popularly associated with Romanticism, and Pope is clearly not a Romantic. But neither was he concerned with the classicism of the 17th century which would have linked him to Lorrain and Poussin. In his witty burlesque poem, *The Rape of the Lock,* written in heroic couplets he settled the score with the world of Ariosto and Baroque hero-worship as early as 1712. In his later works, too, Pope was interested not in individual characters but rather in general questions of "morality", "virtue" and "dangers of

Mellerstain House, Berwickshire, Scotland

A large area of lawn leads from the gardens beside the house to a lake surrounded by woods. The lake was originally laid out in the form of a Dutch *gracht* but is no longer recognizable as such.

231

criticism". It was in the same spirit that he wrote, in 1733–34, his *Essay on Man*, a definitive reflection upon human existence: nature is the only truly passable way for mankind, but will only lead the traveller to his destination of he relinquishes passion and allows himself to be guided by the power of virtue. To Pope the ideal state was one in which "body" and "mind" formed a natural whole and gave shape to their permanent bond in "art":

> Th' Eternal Art educing good from ill,
> Grafts on this Passion our best principle:
> 'Tis thus the Mercury of Man is fixed,
> Strong grows the Virtue with his nature mixed;
> The dross cements what else were too refined,
> And in one interest body acts with mind.
> (*Essay on man*, Epistle II)

Pope himself took the step from literature to garden design, and William Kent with him. Since his real interest was "mankind in general", we should see in the deliberate placing of a solitary tree not an individual tree but rather a "tree absolute", in other words a natural and simultaneously spiritual generality. The English garden is a *monadically* ordered world, formed from simple and indestructible elements. Every single tree is a closed unit, whereby its insulation arises not from external fencing but rather from inner fullness. Each monad is also a reflection of universal wholeness. Thus the idea of a wood no longer requires the actual large-scale planting of a trees. The monadic tree achieves the same effect, if one only knows how to place it and perceive it in the correct way. This is precisely the task of garden design, and is true not just for a tree but also for a meadow, a house, a stream, a cow. Each individual thing, with its carefully-staged solitude pointing to universal relationships of nature, becomes a window onto a *world theatre* containing an infinite number of stages next to, above and below each other. On each of these stages even the smallest object can tell its individual cosmic story.

Anecdote relates that Leibniz one day went for a walk with Princess Sophie-Charlotte through the park at Herrenhausen and asked her to show him two leaves which were identical to each other. She was unable to do so and he was thus able to demonstrate the infinite diversity of nature, which was never so unimaginative as to repeat itself. This infinity, everywhere visible in real shapes, led Leibniz in his *Monadologia* of 1714, to describe the creator of all things as an architect who had placed his creatures with divine foresight on larger and smaller stages and had given each and every one of them the right to be a living reflection, a *point de vue* of the universe.

Monadic ideas are particularly illuminating in the case of the first phase of English garden design. The garden at Stowe is an outstanding example of the lively interaction between the two fundamental principles: identity and reason, mathematical rigour and freedom based on contingency. Its ground-plan demonstrates the confrontation of a strict system of coordinates of straight axes and pathways with the new system of winding lines. The result shows that the two harmonize excellently. But Kent went further and used the Elysian Fields as a stage on which to depict the struggle between Vice and Virtue, one of the favourite themes of his friend Alexander Pope. He set the traditional virtues, dating back to classical antiquity, against the degeneration of the modern age, and unmaster it as the corruption of the present. On the far bank of a river called the Styx he offers a promising view of the heroes of the nation: the British Worthies. Instead of tragedy, therefore, we have a piece of comforting and encouraging political theatre staged within the conciliatoriness of a nature championing truth and goodness.

Two further aspects of the English idea of a garden landscape deserve closer attention, since they also had an influence on fundamental decisions in French and Italian architecture and underline the differences between the various positions.

The first is the idea of *space*. Bramante, in his dividing of the unit of the Belvedere courtyard into three levels, subordinated individual space to the clearly-delimited area of art. Le Nôtre extended space to a cosmic world scale by replacing Bramante's tripartite system with a never-ending series which could only attain appropriate generality and thus its conclusion in the "Absolute". English garden architecture went one step further and yet at the same time returned to "earth" from the realms of the absolute. It made the level of the Belvedere, the panorama the view, into a *universal quantity*. "Universality" is the highest point of generality, which can only be captured when the absolute is brought back from the distant realms it occupies within the framework of particularity to the individual where it is understood to be a "representational" power which can produce reality. It is in this step that we may identify the English turning away from the French conception of nature. The result was a monadic world. The monad is the real centre of universality. It is individual, absolutely separate from everything else and yet can "represent" the whole universe if it can sufficiently actualize that which is contained within it. Leibniz compared the interdependence of all monads with a stone falling into the sea. The effect of the waves produced extends not just to the immediate area but to the furthest points of the sea. In this way is possible to indeed understand space as a universal quantity in which every position relates to every other.

Architecture made use of this unlimitedness of space by reproducing, in the garden of a London villa, the Pantheon from Rome, a villa rotunda in the Palladian style or a temple from Agrigas. Once one has recognized the presence of the monadic idea, transforming an individual garden into a universal landscape, there can no longer be any talk of ecleticism or cultural middle-class. The concept of "representation" acquires new significance here. Perception and thinking are not just physiological activities which connect the internal with the external. They have the power to fetch things not immediately available from their relative remoteness into the direct present. This takes place on thought; but since the thinking of a monad is also always propulsion into reality, represented things appear in real form in designed nature and bring into the universal dialogue of the landscape the spiritual power within them.

The gardens at Rousham and Stourhead are convincing examples of how a park can be a "world stage", on which the unity of natural and spiritual universality can bind even the most disparate parts into a harmonious landscape. This aspect was taken to perhaps its furthest extreme by William Chambers in his designs for Kew Gardens, with its famous pagoda, house of Confucius, Gothic cathedral, Alhambra and Turkish mosque. Their close proximity led to Chambers' being mockingly accused

Packwood House, Warwickshire, England

The garden at Packwood was laid out in the middle of the 19th century. Although it cannot strictly be described as a landscape garden, it lies as an enclosed area within a beautiful landscape setting.

of presenting "the whole world in one hectare". He was also frequently criticized for the miniature format of his replicas. But it is precisely this which reveals that he was interested not in the imitation of real buildings but rather in the representation of their immanent ideational power.

The second idea which should be emphasized is that of *time*, which belongs directly with that of space. The French gave space and time a parallelism which expressed itself as an infinite line striving for the absolute. The English had as little interest in such a purpose-oriented linearity as in counterchecking the two within a system of other-directional coordinates. If time is also to be universally embraced, it must be expanded and joined to form a *circle*, in which not only the periphery but the entire surface area has a temporal dimension.

Considering the English garden from this point of view one is no longer surprised by the enormous and often courageous leaps in time which can be found within one landscape: an Egyptian obelisk, Greek columns, a Gothic ruin, houses in the style of classical antiquity and – again and again – the Vestal temple from Tivoli. They stand in harmonious juxtaposition, with no linear idea of history requiring them to compete with each other. The universal understanding of history initiated here, interested neither in the beginning nor the end of history, but solely in the equal gathering of all eras, led eventually to the *encyclopédistes* who began working on their comprehensive summaries of the whole of culture as from the middle of the century.

Packwood House, Warwickshire, England
The brick wall planted with flowers forms the edge of a terrace; it separates the upper from the lower part of the garden.

In the opinion of many, however, the real pinnacle of English landscape gardening was not reached until a second phase, whose most distinguished exponent was Lancelot "Capability" Brown. The term "phase" does not necessarily imply a chronological sequence. It is rather a question of two different methods of construing landscape.

The first phase could be described as that of the *idealists*. These included Pope, Burlington, Kent, Shenstone and Brown's greatest competitor, William Chambers. This phase was characterized by the great value which it placed on spiritual elements. Thus they populated their landscapes with meaningful pieces of architecture, specified precise prospects and at times provided commentaries on their vistas in the form of plaques with erudite inscriptions.

The second phase, that of Capability Brown, can rightly be described as that of the *naturalists*. Brown banned educational elements from his landscapes and avoided built architecture as far as possible. It is often claimed that the "classic" English landscape garden contains no architecture, only nature. But this point of view forgets that even "nature" is the work of an architect. Brown knew this very well and took upon himself the challenge of that "First Architect".

He always described his own work very modestly as "improvement". He wished only to improve, refine, accentuate, rearrange and rectify existing faults. And yet he was always very aware that he was working on a "construction" as an architect of nature. Michelangelo's *Last Judge-*

235

ment had shown that it was perfectly possible to do without pillars, vaults and other architectural elements and to design space via the simple arrangement of bodies. In the palace at Würzburg, Brown's contemporary Tiepolo achieved a triumph of spatial perspective design analogous to Brown's own landscapes, without employing built architecture. Modest as his claim sounded, the standard was high: Lancelot Brown was the "Second Architect", and he had nature in his power. That he was very aware of the competitiveness of his situation is demonstrated by a characteristic remark in which he said that the River Thames would never forgive him if it could see the artificial lake which he had created at Blenheim.

His course of action was always the same, and it earned him the curious nickname of "Capability". He was convinced that natural conditions could only be improved if the architect started from the "capabilities" inherent in the landscape. Some people like to interpret "capabilities" as "possibilities", but this takes insufficient account of the naturalistic methods of his architecture. It was the idealists, such as his rival Chambers, who filled their landscapes with "possible" temples, churches and pagodas. Leibniz coined an important, here more appropriate concept in his *exis-titurire* or "propelling into existence". This is where Brown takes up. Every landscape has natural dispositions and capabilities which press to the fore because they release more reality than others. It is the task of the architect to ensure that a maximum of nature is created. Is this not better left up to nature itself? Clearly not. Capability Brown set himself up directly beside the Architect of the Universe and made himself master of those realities propelling themselves into existence. Remembering the universal claim of idea of the English garden, then one understands why the last walls and fences had to fall before Lancelot Brown. No boundary now exists which can constrain "Second Nature". Thus it extends to the barn, the river and the distant features of the landscape. In his over 200 parks, Capability Brown "redesigned" almost the whole of southern and central England. He could be satisfied with the result; he had, after all, succeeded in transforming a vast region into a theatre landscape on which just one drama was played:

The Fall and the Rise of Nature.

Rievaulx Terrace, North Yorkshire, England
Gothic ruins of Rievaulx Abbey

Not far from Studley Royal lies Rievaulx Terrace, a terraced area on the edge of a steep slope which is bordered by one Ionic and one Doric temple. From here there is a splendid view of Rievaulx Abbey. Such monumental testaments to the Middle Ages had tremendous cult value for the Romantics among the English garden architects who gained influence in the latter part of the 18th century.

Map of garden sites

Italy
1. Villa d'Este, Tivoli
2. Villa Aldobrandini, Frascati
3. Palazzina Farnese, Caprarola
4. Villa Lante, Bagnaia
5. Bomarzo
6. Boboli Gardens, Florence
7. Villa Gamberaia, Settignano
8. Villa il Bosco di Fonte Lucente, Fiesole
9. Villa Garzoni, Collodi

Germany
10. Schwetzingen
11. Weikersheim
12. Veitshöchheim
13. Hermitage, Bayreuth
14. Sanspareil, Bayreuth
15. Brühl
16. Herrenhausen, Hanover
17. Charlottenburg, Berlin

Austria
18. Belvedere, Vienna
19. Schönbrunn, Vienna
20. Laxenburg, near Vienna
21. Hellbrunn, Salzburg
22. Kleßheim, Salzburg

Netherlands
23. Het Loo, Apeldoorn
24. Rosendael, Arnhem

France
25. Versailles
26. Vaux-le-Vicomte, near Melun
27. Villandry, near Tours

England
28. Stourhead, Wiltshire
29. Petworth, West Sussex
30. Blenheim, Oxfordshire
31. Stowe, Buckinghamshire
32. Packwood House, Warwickshire
33. Chatsworth, Derbyshire
34. Studley Royal, North Yorkshire
35. Rievaulx Terrace, North Yorkshire
36. Castle Howard, North Yorkshire

Scotland
37. Mellerstain, Gordon, Berwickshire

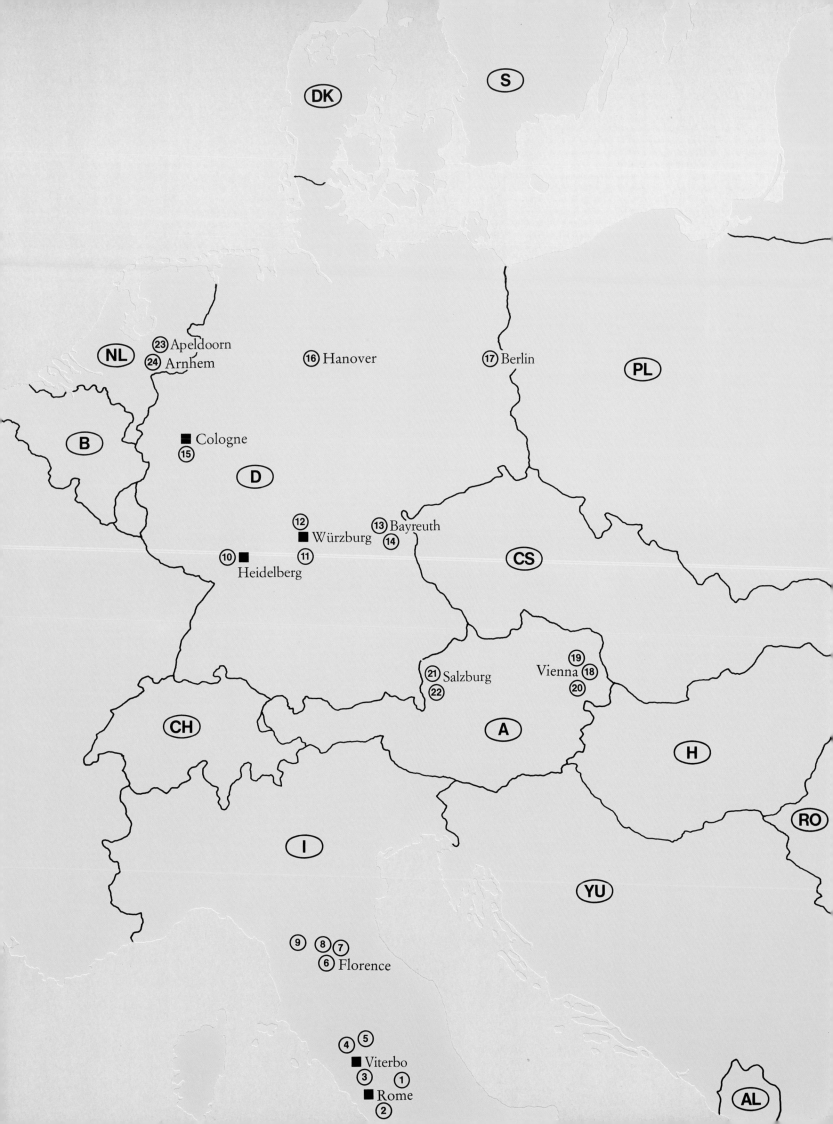

DK

S

NL ㉓ Apeldoorn
㉔ Arnhem

⑯ Hanover

⑰ Berlin

PL

B

■ Cologne
⑮

D

⑫
■ Würzburg
⑬ Bayreuth
⑭

CS

⑩ ■
Heidelberg
⑪

㉑ Salzburg
㉒

⑲
Vienna ⑱
⑳

CH

A

H

RO

I

YU

⑨ ⑧ ⑦
⑥ Florence

④ ⑤
■ Viterbo
③ ①
■ Rome
②

AL

470.000,-

Photographic acknowledgements:
Martin Claßen photographed the Italian, German and Dutch gardens, and
Hans Wiesenhofer the French, English and Austrian gardens.

Hans Wiesenhofer works with Minolta-AF cameras and Minolta-AF lenses.

Source of black-and-white illustrations:
Archiv für Kunst und Geschichte, Berlin: p. 133
Bayerische Verwaltung der Staatl. Schlösser, Gärten und Seen, Munich: p. 149
Bildarchiv Preußischer Kulturbesitz, Berlin: p. 141
Mary Evans Picture Library, London: p. 9, 13, 31, 108, 186, 187, 192, 198, 199, 204, 212
The National Trust/Photographic Library, London: p. 213
The remaining illustrations are taken from the archives of the publisher and the authors.